Classic Restaurants
of
BOSTON

ZACHARY LAMOTHE

AMERICAN PALATE

Published by American Palate
A Division of The History Press
Charleston, SC
www.historypress.com

All cover images by Jaclyn Lamothe except Union Oyster House, courtesy of Joseph Milano, and Cheers, by Ann Marie Lyons.

First published 2021

Manufactured in the United States

ISBN 9781467147057

Library of Congress Control Number: 2021943538

To Jackie, my number one "traveling companion"

Contents

Contents

Acknowledgements

I would like to thank the following friends and family members who pointed me to certain classic Boston restaurants that just had to be included in this collection: Bob Gallagher, Meaghan and James Hutchinson, Greg Levings and Paula Mack. A tip of the cap in thanks to Joseph and Kricket Milano for sharing all of their wonderful photos of Union Oyster House to be used in the book. Thanks to Mary DiLeo from All Heart PR for the Anna's Taqueria photos by Brian Samuels. A round of applause for Ann Marie and David Lyons, who not only had suggestions but also became field photographers of a few Boston restaurants at the height of the pandemic. Thanks to Jocelyn Moschella for my author photo.

To my kids, Danny and Tommy, thanks for usually understanding when I needed to take a break from playtime to write. A truly heartfelt thanks to my wife, Jackie, who in four books' time has gone from "traveling companion" to primary photographer. Thanks to my mom, forever the English teacher, who has been my proofreader since day one. Thanks to both of my parents for taking me to many of these classic Boston restaurants and introducing me to the city as a kid. And thanks to Mike Kinsella, my editor, who believed this project would be a good fit for me.

Introduction

A major part of what defines a city is its cuisine. A variety of foods are associated with the city of Boston and its environs. Throughout the history of the city, from its colonial roots to the current day, food has played a significant role in Boston. Boston itself is nicknamed for a prized legume, "Beantown." As much as Boston is known for its distinct menu items, the Greater Boston area, from the North Shore to the South Shore, also has its share of regional specialties, including the roast beef sandwich, the bar pizza and the fried clam. Of course, with its coastal locale, seafood favorites such as New England clam chowder, or "chowda" as the locals say, lobster rolls and scrod are also on the menu. From the first Thanksgiving to the present day, food has followed closely with the history of the Boston region.

The story of cuisine in the Boston area starts in 1620 with the arrival of the group known to history as the Pilgrims, just down the road in Plymouth. This book winds through the founding of the Massachusetts Bay Colony and Boston, through its colonial and Revolutionary War era, and encompasses waves of immigration up to the twenty-first century. From the Union Oyster House and Parker's Restaurant to Legal Sea Foods and Regina Pizzeria, classic restaurants have become synonymous with the city of Boston. Known for a wide variety of food, from baked goods to burritos and seafood to spaghetti, a visit to Boston would not be complete without stopping at these classic restaurants.

PART I

THE HISTORY OF BOSTON FOOD

Boston Cuisine through the Years

THE ROOTS OF BOSTON FOOD

Upon the arrival of the English Separatists (historically known as the Pilgrims) in 1620 and the establishment of the Plymouth Colony, the region now known as Massachusetts would be forever changed. The event took place thirty-five miles from Boston, but the idea of the "First Thanksgiving" between the English and the Wampanoag tribe has been ingrained in the lore of this country. Although it was hardly a Thanksgiving as we celebrate today, analyzing this event is a great place to start in understanding the food of the English arrivals and the area's Native peoples. One group's menu choices were completely dependent on what was available locally and in season, while the other brought with them English traditions that had to be adapted to a new lifestyle and geography.

The First Thanksgiving occurred in the fall of 1621, with scholars pinpointing it between September 21 and November 9 in the Wampanoag village of Patuxet (Plymouth). It was a three-day feast, with venison being the main dish. Of course, it has only been deemed the "First Thanksgiving" in retrospect. In actuality, it was a harvest festival or a "harvest home." Little is known of this actual event since it was only mentioned through the words of Edward Winslow and William Bradford. Winslow's account here is through a letter written on December 11, 1621:

Our harvest being gotten in, our governor sent four men on fowling, that so we might after a special manner rejoice together, after we had gathered the fruits of our labors; they four in one day killed as much fowl, as with a little help beside, served the Company almost a week, at which time amongst other Recreations, we exercised our arms, many of the Indians coming amongst us, and amongst the rest their greatest king Massasoit, with some ninety men, whom for three days we entertained and feasted, and they went out and killed five deer, which they brought to the Plantation and bestowed on our Governor, and upon the Captain and others. And although it be not always so plentiful, as it was at this time with us, yet by the goodness of God, we are so far from want, that we often wish you partakers of our plenty.

Of course, the typical "fowl" that we associate with Thanksgiving is turkey. Yes, wild turkeys were prevalent (and still are) in this region of Massachusetts. Other fowl that were typically eaten included geese and ducks and even crane and eagle. Another major source of protein was deer meat, called venison, which was brought to the feast by the Wampanoag. Other popular foods associated with Thanksgiving include the cranberry, which is also native to this region of Massachusetts. Cranberry sauce, either canned or homemade, is doctored up with a good amount of sugar used on today's table. Cranberries could have been eaten during this feast, since they are in season in the fall, but would not have been heightened with the use of sugar. Potatoes would not have been on the menu since they were not native, but pumpkin and squash could have been. There was no Bell's stuffing, but the fowl could have been stuffed with wild onions, oats and herbs.

Winslow also mentioned other foods that were found in the Plymouth region, including many types of fish (including eel); shellfish such as lobsters, mussels and oysters; and fruit such as plums, strawberries and grapes. Vegetables included carrots, cabbage, turnips and onions. The major food planted by the Native peoples was known as the "Three Sisters": corn, beans and squash. The corn, also called maize, was very different from the large ears that we slather with butter, cover with salt and sink our teeth into. What has become known as "Indian corn," with hard kernels of different colors, was what was grown. It actually still grows in the Plymouth area today. This was ground and used in various products, including porridge. Although Winslow's records come from the Plymouth Colony, with its proximity to present-day Boston, the bounty of the sea and the forest, as well as the items brought over by its English settlers, would be similar to the food that would also help establish the Massachusetts Bay Colony at Boston in 1630.

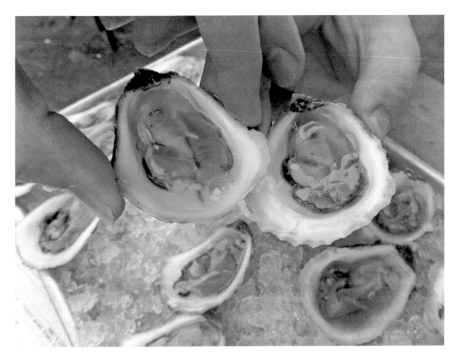

Oysters are one of the many gifts of the sea that Boston is known for. *Jaclyn Lamothe.*

In addition, other foods grown included parsnips, radishes, muskmelons, cucumbers and herbs, such as marjoram, sarsaparilla and yarrow. Typical fruits were strawberries, gooseberries, blueberries, raspberries, currants and huckleberries. This was similar to the colonists' diet in England. Many varieties of fish could be found in the fresh and salt waters of Massachusetts. These included freshwater alewives (herring), mackerel, salmon, bass, halibut, shad, cod and, in the salt water, eels, oysters, lobsters and clams.

Deer were a popular animal to eat, but many others were consumed also, including bears, moose, wolves, raccoons, otters, skunks and beavers. Deer was a delicacy or celebratory food. For most Native peoples of the region, 70 percent of their diet consisted of corn and beans. Although meat comes to mind as a major component of a meal, ironically, meat only made up less than 20 percent of the diet of Native peoples, with other items such as vegetables/plants, berries, eggs, fish and shellfish making up the final 10 percent.

Corn was turned into many uses for Native peoples, including being used for a food called *nocake*. The corn was smothered in hot ashes and then ground into a powder. It was a food that, when traveling, was easy to eat and was filling enough to suppress hunger. Dried corn flour was also used as a thickener for soups.

Upon settling, the English learned growing techniques from the Wampanoag, including using fish such as herring as fertilizer for crops, as well as drying and smoking food. The English soon raised crops and tended gardens. Corn was an all-important crop for the new arrivals, as it was for the Native population. Women typically tended the gardens and grew parsley, lettuce, spinach, carrots and turnips, along with other vegetables.

In England, the most popular beverage to drink (even for kids) was beer. Water was oftentimes unsafe to drink. Although beer was brought over on the *Mayflower*, the colonists did not have brewing methods initially. They opted to drink spring water instead. Mint, ginger or sassafras could be added to flavor the water and enjoyed as a hot drink. Alcoholic beverages such as cider would soon take hold in the colonies as well. As the colonies grew, cider became the most popular drink by the mid-seventeenth century, with John Adams reporting that he enjoyed a glass every morning. Cider is in reference to alcoholic hard cider, not the sweetened cider found at the grocery store today.

From 1620 onward, it was a clash of two cultures ideologically, politically, religiously and even gastronomically. One group relied on the season and

Plymouth Rock commemorates the landing of the Pilgrims. *Author's photo.*

local ingredients, and the other had old-world traditions. With learning the customs of the Native people, a crop such as corn promoted global change. Through the Columbian Exchange, which is the interchange of ideas, foods, disease and technology across continents, corn would become one of the most popular crops worldwide.

Eventually, traditional gastronomic fare from Europe was brought over and adapted to the landscape of New England. Cattle, potatoes and apples were introduced and rapidly changed the diet of the region. English customs included the enclosure of land for raising livestock and cutting down trees for farmable land. The traditions of the Native people were to live harmoniously with nature, only taking what was necessary without drastically changing their surroundings.

THE FOUNDING OF BOSTON

Boston was founded in 1630. A year earlier, the Massachusetts Bay Colony was established up the coast from the Plymouth Colony. Boston would be its major outpost. The first settler, William Blackstone, moved to what would become Boston after arriving in 1623 in Weymouth, the second English settlement founded in New England after Plymouth. Blackstone lived in what is now known as Beacon Hill and famously sold a parcel of land to the Puritan settlers in 1630, which thus established Boston Common. Similar to Plymouth, the land of Boston was populated for thousands of years by Native peoples, but due to the Great Dying, the area became devoid of people. The Great Dying was the decimation of the Native peoples due to widespread disease between 1616 and 1619.

Blackstone planted apple trees near his Boston home. Another famous fruit with Boston ties is the pear. Years later, in England, a pear variety known as the Williams pear was grown in Roxbury. Eventually, this property was sold to Enoch Bartlett, and from then on, it has been known as the Bartlett pear.

The group of Puritans who were to establish the Massachusetts Bay Colony had to decide what foods to bring with them. Their packing list included fruits such as peaches, plums, cherries, apples and pears; grains such as wheat, barley, rye and oats; and vegetables, including potatoes, peas and beans. The first major industry in Boston centered on food: cod fishing. The waters were plentiful with this white fish. The "sacred cod," a wood-carved codfish, hangs in the Massachusetts State House over the building's Senate chamber.

BEANTOWN

Boston has many nicknames, including "the Hub of the Universe" or "the Hub" for short, penned by Oliver Wendell Holmes. The Shining City upon a Hill is another name for Boston given by founder Jonathan Winthrop in a sermon given before arriving in the colony, for he believed this colony would be an example to all future civilizations. Other nicknames for the city are "Cradle of Liberty," due to its part in the American Revolution, and, more recently, "Title Town" for the many championships that its sports teams have won over the last few years.

"Beantown" is the most referenced, however, and it may seem curious since Boston and beans do not have much of a commonality presently. The bean, with roots in the Puritan tradition, is often associated with the New England Yankee custom of eating baked beans and brown bread, especially on Saturday night. It even led to the popularity of bean dinners at churches. Beans were grown by Native people, with the legume's roots harkening back to South America. Pork originated in the colonies with the arrival of pigs from England. A sauce made with molasses appeared during the eighteenth century's triangular trade, along with brown bread made with rye mixed into the cornmeal.

Through the history of the region to the present, food and its traditions have always been an integral part of the culture of Boston and its surroundings. Welcome to a culinary trek through the streets and suburbs of Boston as we explore its classic restaurants and its most popular dishes.

A WORD BEFORE WE EAT

This book was primarily written during the COVID-19 pandemic. As with almost all facets of life, the effects of the pandemic permanently altered Boston's classic restaurant scene. Longtime eating establishments shuttered, not able to weather the COVID storm. At the time of the writing of this book, the restaurants included in this book are operational, but unfortunately, current status is subject to change. Even if they make it through the pandemic intact, there is no question that the restaurant industry is still reeling. Now is a better time than ever to go out and show your support for these and other classic and non-classic restaurants, whether for dine in or takeout. The following chapters identify some of Boston's most classic restaurants by date, by neighborhood or by cuisine, as well as others located in the Boston 'burbs.

PART II

THE BOSTON CLASSICS

Union Oyster House

1826

Many establishments claim to be the oldest continuously run restaurant in America. The Union Oyster House also makes this claim. Verifiable or not, the Union Oyster House is emphatically a classic Boston restaurant and has been shucking, with its patrons slurping, the briny bivalves since 1826. It's located at 41 Union Street, right on the Freedom Trail and a short walk from landmarks such as Faneuil Hall, Government Center and the North End. With its large block letter sign perched atop the building facing toward the North End, it's easy to locate this Boston institution.

The building itself is one of the oldest in Boston, built in the Georgian architectural style in the years 1716 and 1717. Georgian architecture's emphasis is on classical symmetry and proportion. It is the oldest brick building of this design in the city. Prior to being known for its oysters, over one hundred years of history already took place here. It was a dress shop known as At the Sign of the Cornfields. Future King of France Louis Phillippe I lived upstairs in the building while in exile from France. Also located here was the political newspaper the *Massachusetts Spy*, printed and published by Isaiah Thomas, which was one of the first newspapers in America. He printed it here between the years 1771 and 1775 upon fleeing Boston for Worcester. Thomas is also known for the first public oration of the Declaration of Independence and founding the American Antiquarian Society.

In 1826, the Atwood and Bacon Oyster House was born. By 1916, it had become known by its current moniker, Union Oyster House. Fewer than

Union Oyster House is the classic Boston restaurant. *Courtesy of Joseph Milano.*

a handful of owners have been at the helm of the Union Oyster House, including the Fitzgerald family and the Greaves brothers; during their tenure, they owned other branches of Union Oyster Houses in the city. The current owners are Joseph A. Milano Jr. and Mary Ann Milano Picardi, who have been carrying on the historic oyster house's traditions since 1970. The interior, with its dark walls and ceiling, outlines Boston history, with depictions of the Freedom Trail stops (that this restaurant is part of!). The famous semicircular oyster bar commemorates Daniel Webster.

In addition to being one of those "have to visit spots" in Boston, the oyster house has won many accolades over the years. It was named by the travel guide *Lonely Planet* as one of the "500 Best Restaurants in the World" in 2018. Also in 2018, *Condé Nast Traveler* proclaimed it as one of Boston's best restaurants, and *USA Today* selected it as the home of Boston's best clam chowder. It also earned a historically significant recognition in 2003 as a National Historic Landmark. A fun fact is that the toothpick was first used here.

The Atwood and Bacon Oyster House. *Courtesy of Joseph Milano.*

Many celebrities and politicians have been patrons of the restaurant over the years. The public figure with the most known ties to the restaurant is John F. Kennedy, who even had his own booth. Booth 18 today features a plaque to the Massachusetts-born president. He often enjoyed a quiet Sunday meal of lobster soup. The Kennedy family ate at the Union Oyster House often. Statesman Daniel Webster, though, had the most profound reputation around these parts. The politician would consume an average

The interior of Union Oyster House from a bygone era. *Courtesy of Joseph Milano.*

of six plates of half a dozen oysters daily, along with a tumbler of brandy and water. Other celebrities who have graced the booths or bar of the Union Oyster House include Franklin Delano Roosevelt, Steven Spielberg, Meryl Streep, Paul Newman, Ozzy Osbourne, Larry Bird, Robert Redford and Luciano Pavarotti. Unveiled in 2003 by artist D. Hummel-Marconi, a celebrity-laden painting graces the wall of Union Oyster House, featuring guests of the restaurant, including Bobby Orr, Jay Leno and Muhammad Ali, among many others listed here.

John R. Coleman, the president of Haverford College in Pennsylvania and the chairman of Philadelphia's Federal Reserve, took a sabbatical in 1973, during which he was employed in various positions in the country. One of them was as a sandwich maker at Union Oyster House. His yearlong sabbatical was turned into a book the following year.

Throughout its history as well as in the present day, the Union Oyster House has been known for its oysters, served raw, grilled and fried, as well as the prime ingredient in Oysters Rockefeller. Other Boston specialties such as the lobster dinner and lobster roll are served, as well as scrod and Boston baked beans. The menu consists of many seafood options, but there is a variety of landlubber favorites as well, including chicken and steak.

To bring back a souvenir from your visit to Union Oyster House, stop by Union Goods at the restaurant. It's a gift shop full of all things Union Oyster House–related, including clothing, trinkets and other memorabilia.

Parker's Restaurant

1855

Located inside the iconic Omni Parker House at 60 School Street, which heralds itself as the oldest continuously run hotel in the country, is arguably one of the most famous restaurants in Boston: Parker's Restaurant. Actually, Parker's would be on the shortlist for most important restaurants in the country. Where else are three classic dishes associated with the same restaurant? It is the ultimate classic Boston restaurant.

The Parker House Hotel was built in 1854 and opened to the public a year later on October 8, 1855. For the chic hotel, built by Harvey D. Parker, a fine-dining eatery was needed to accompany it. The restaurant is adorned in oak and complemented by fine crystal chandeliers. With its high ceilings and white tablecloths, it has an air of importance.

The restaurant is known for three different Boston-associated dishes: Boston cream pie, Parker House rolls and scrod. The Boston cream pie has been deemed the official dessert of Massachusetts. It is a yellow cake layered with custard and topped by a coating of dark chocolate icing. Created by French Parker House chef Augustine Francois Anezin in the nineteenth century, this delectable treat has become closely associated with the city of Boston.

Another Parker House creation is the Parker House roll. This restaurant staple has its roots in the 1870s. The legend says that a disgruntled worker baked unfinished rolls after an argument with a guest, thus giving the roll its indented shape with its crispy outside and soft interior.

Scrod is not an actual fish. For high-end restaurants such as Parker's, it was vital to make sure the fish they served was the freshest. This is the legend of

The façade of the Omni Parker House, location of Parker's Restaurant. *Jaclyn Lamothe.*

the scrod. Not knowing exactly what type of fish would be at the top of the heap, literally, the Parker House would demand the top of the fisherman's daily catch from the wharves of Boston since it was the freshest. A Parker House maître d' used the word *scrod* no matter what kind of fish, whether it be cod, halibut or pollock. Although the tale of the origin of the word *scrod* may be the stuff of legend, Parker House takes pride in its creation, along with its world-famous pie and rolls.

Along with its important dishes, Parker's Restaurant has had its share of important figures walk through its corridors. The Parker House was the meeting place of a group of elite individuals on each Saturday of the month, known as the Saturday Club. The group included such dignitaries as Ralph Waldo Emerson, John Greenleaf Whittier, Henry David Thoreau and Henry Wadsworth Longfellow, with some as regular attendees and others occasional. Others who traveled through or stayed at the hotel for a period of time joined the group and included such iconic figures as Charles Dickens and Mark Twain. This was the site of Dickens's first reading of *A Christmas Carol* and Longfellow's of "The Midnight Ride of Paul Revere."

Presidents such as John F. Kennedy, Bill Clinton and Ulysses S. Grant have been guests. The Parker House has also had its share of historic employees. Ho Chi Minh, the revolutionary and eventual leader of North Vietnam, was employed as a baker at the Parker House between the years 1912 and 1913. Malcolm Little, better known as Malcolm X, worked at the Parker House as part of the waitstaff during the early 1940s. Current executive chef Gerry Tice is lauded in his own right, while former chefs who have worked here include Chef Emeril Lagasse as sous chef from 1979 to 1981. Other celebrity chefs who have honed their skills in the kitchen of the Parker House include Lydia Shire and Jasper White.

For Boston history on a plate, look no further than the Parker's Restaurant in the famed Omni Parker Hotel. And while you're there, try to request table 40. It is where John F. Kennedy proposed to his future wife, Jacqueline Bouvier. The Parker House is located at 60 School Street in the heart of downtown Boston.

SPOTLIGHT ON: CHEF EMERIL LAGASSE

Chef Lagasse, better known to his legions of culinary fans as simply "Emeril," is closely associated with the Cajun-style cuisine of New Orleans. As a true celebrity chef, Emeril's fame comes from not only his namesake restaurants and vast number of cookbooks but also his many appearances on television shows. Unbeknownst to many, Lagasse is actually from Massachusetts. He was born and raised in Fall River and went to culinary school at Johnson and Wales University in Providence, Rhode Island. His ties to Boston include his stint as a sous chef in the kitchen of Parker's Restaurant. He has been named

"Chef of the Year," and his restaurants have won numerous accolades, starting with Emeril's, which opened in New Orleans in 1990. As a true celebrity chef of the cable TV era, Lagasse is known for his catchphrases, including "Bam!" Currently, his list of eateries includes four restaurants in New Orleans and other outposts in Pennsylvania, Las Vegas and Florida; all are unique and distinct from each other. Even though he is closely associated with New Orleans and what he calls "New New Orleans" cooking, his roots are in Massachusetts.

The Marliave

1875/1885

Although it has not been in continuous operation, Marliave's history dates back to the late nineteenth century. In the twenty-first century, it is just as viable and up-to-date as it was almost 150 years ago. It prides itself on being the "oldest chef-owned restaurant in Boston." The Marliave was the dream of Parisian-American immigrant Henry Marliave. His namesake restaurant became an institution. It is located at 10 Bosworth Street, which doubles as an alleyway, in the heart of Downtown Crossing. The menu is a mix of French and Italian fare with a modern flair. The emphasis at Marliave is freshness. The freshest meats, seafood and vegetables are served here. The French cassoulet, beef Wellington and lobster Thermidor are incredibly popular. It was reopened by Scott Herritt, who is also at the helm of Grotto, the popular Beacon Hill restaurant. Scallops, salmon and the raw bar are ever-popular. The first level is the (alcohol) bar and cappuccino bar, with the second floor reserved for fine dining. It is also a popular wedding venue. The black-and-white theme is prevalent throughout the restaurant, from its façade to its interior.

The Marliave, one of Boston's oldest restaurants. *Jaclyn Lamothe*.

Amrheins

1890

Amrheins in South Boston has brought many firsts to the city. Credit goes to Amrheins for the first draft beer pump in Boston. Another accolade includes its gorgeous hand-carved bar, which claims to be the oldest in the country. Additionally, in a neighborhood synonymous with bars and pubs, Amrheins is said to be the oldest. Amrheins is known for its take on comfort food, including sandwiches, seafood and salad. Recently, it has updated its menu to reflect its position in a revitalized Southie. The new menu is proud to have ingredients that are locally sourced and a large variety of items.

The dining room at Amrheins was once a funeral parlor, and the restaurant has been known as a political hangout over the years. No matter how Southie has changed, what has not is the fact that Amrheins is a classic neighborhood restaurant where the patrons cannot get enough of their dishes. From salads to steak, everyone will find something to their liking at the restaurant.

First-time patrons are wowed by the intricately designed wooden bar. This was brought here by the Amrhein brothers from Austria. The beautiful long bar includes a polished marble countertop. On the walls are historic photos. The restaurant sits on the first floor of a four-story attractive brick building at 80 West Broadway. Although the address is not far from downtown Boston, it has a distinctly neighborhood feel. The current owner of Amrheins is Steve Mulrey. His father, Joseph, started Mul's Diner, located across the street, over seventy-five years ago. The family still owns Mul's today.

In addition to serving the mealtime and bar crowd, Amrheins provides outdoor seating and is a popular function facility.

Santarpio's Pizza

1903

There is a rivalry in town that goes back almost as far as the Red Sox versus the Yankees. What's the best pizza: Santarpio's Pizza in East Boston or Regina Pizzeria in the North End? Boston-area pizza aficionados are either team Santarpio or team Regina. Santarpio's started as a bakery in East Boston or "Eastie" in 1903 by Italian immigrant Francisco "Frank" Santarpio, who began selling pizza for those in need of something to eat after consuming too much wine. The pizza started being sold in earnest in 1933.

Santarpio's is located at 111 Chelsea Street in East Boston in a nondescript three-story building. The restaurant is on the ground floor, with pale brick marking the front of it. The best-known feature of the building is the large, wide "Santarpio's Pizza" sign adorning the front. The man in the sign is none other than Joe Fats, or Joseph Timpone, uncle to the current owner, Frank Santarpio, who was so named due to his portly nature. Timpone's recipe for their pizza is what is served today. When Prohibition was repealed, Santarpio's changed from a bakery to a bar that sold lunchtime fare, with Timpone manning the pizza oven in the evening.

The pizza recipe was just as Timpone liked it, including the crispiness of the pie. It's a thin-crust pizza, which is familiarly called New York style, but owner Frank Santarpio cautions against giving it a style. Instead, Santarpio describes his pizza simply as dough, tomatoes and cheese. The third generation of Santarpios took the helm in 1966. When Frank took over the family business, he redid the interior, and that is how it looks

The iconic sign looming over Santarpio's in East Boston. *Jaclyn Lamothe.*

today. The no-frills establishment is lined with booths and has a bar. The only items on the menu are pizza, steak tips, lamb tips and sausage. They also serve crusty bread, which customers can rip off in chunks to create an impromptu sandwich.

Not much has changed since the '60s. The pizza choices are basic. The dough is made fresh every day, and Santarpio's style is based on the distinct placement of the toppings. Instead of the toppings being placed on top—hence the name "toppings"—Santarpio's puts them under the layer of cheese. Thus, the order is dough, toppings, cheese and then sauce. The pizza comes out of the oven with a crispiness but is never burned. Popular pizzas include pepperoni; sausage and garlic; and pepperoni, garlic and onion. Other customers swear by their meats and opt for those when visiting Santarpio's.

Santarpio's is often on "Best of Boston" lists in publications such as *Boston Magazine*. It has been featured on Andrew Zimmern's *Bizarre Foods with Andrew Zimmern*. The restaurant website the Daily Meal ranked it the twenty-ninth-best pizza in the United States, and it was also listed by *Food and Wine Magazine* on its list of best pizza places in the United States.

Santarpio's expanded to a second location on Route 1 in Peabody. Although the building is much newer than the Eastie location, the interior is still basic and serves the same dishes. There is also a third branch that opened up in Logan Airport with other favorites such as Kelly's Roast Beef and Sullivan's to showcase the cuisine of Boston neighborhoods.

The interior of Santarpio's is decorated in boxing memorabilia. It is a cash-only establishment. Expect long lines if you visit on a weekend night. Santarpio's is hands down one of the best pizzas, if not the best, found in Boston.

S&S Restaurant

1919

I f you are looking for a classic restaurant with loads of tasty options, you must try S&S Restaurant in Cambridge's Inman Square. For over one hundred years, S&S has fed hordes of hungry diners. Currently operated by the Mitchell and Wheeler family, the name "S&S" is derived from an oft-repeated Yiddish phrase said by great-grandmother Ma Edelstein to patrons entering the restaurant. *Es and es* translates to "eat and eat," the phrase that Ma would relay to the hungry customers.

Often thought of in terms of a deli, S&S Restaurant certainly has delicious deli options but includes so much more than a traditional deli. Corned beef and pastrami are staples of the sandwich board. Choose from one of the many sandwich options or design your own with choice of meat, bread, cheese and accoutrements. The deli options are certainly "old school," with even liver and tongue on the menu. Breakfast choices abound at S&S with omelettes, bagels and blintzes. For something heartier than a sandwich, entrées include rack of lamb, New York sirloin steak and seafood options. Quite frankly, this is an extensive menu. There are even barbecue dishes such as ribs and chicken. Certainly, S&S will please the whole family. Wine and beer are available as well.

S&S is a bit of an anomaly. Cambridge is decidedly a hip city, known for counterculture, underground rock-and-roll and collegiate types. Inman Square is at the heart of the city. Not as chain-heavy as the now-commercialized Harvard Square, Inman still has a true hipster vibe. A long-standing restaurant such as S&S may seem out of place in this neighborhood.

The interior of S&S is reminiscent of a place that grandma might have taken the family. At the same time, the coolness of S&S pervades, showing that some good ideas are timeless. One thing is for sure, at S&S you will not leave hungry. S&S is located at the center of Inman Square at 1334 Cambridge Street in Cambridge.

Winthrop Arms Restaurant

1919

Although Winthrop is a separate city from Boston, its geography makes it unique. The land of Winthrop is a peninsula that sticks out into the harbor just north of Boston. It is actually directly across from Logan Airport. It borders the Boston neighborhood of East Boston and the city of Revere. Being a peninsula, there is no reason to drive through Winthrop en route to anywhere else; the only destination traveling through Winthrop is Winthrop itself. Other than being a picturesque surfside community, one major reason travelers visit Winthrop is the restaurant at the Winthrop Arms Hotel. It is one of the area's oldest, dating back to 1919.

At the Winthrop Arms, expect classic old-fashioned hearty meals and the utmost in customer service. The Winthrop Arms is owned by David Goll, who is known as "The Doctor." Goll can often be seen greeting customers, and he calls each gentleman "doctor." The Winthrop Arms is the real deal in terms of food. Expect generous portions of crowd-pleasing classics such as turkey dinner, salmon, steak tips or New York sirloin. One favorite, named after the good doctor himself, is Doc's Chicken Potpie. Even though Winthrop's seaside location is often thought of in terms of summertime, the food and the cozy dining room make the Winthrop Arms perfect for winter too. The lounge area and bar are conducive to enjoying a few cold brews and an appetizer if a full dinner is not in the plans.

Being connected to the Winthrop Arms Hotel means that if you're too tired after a big meal, you can see if a room is available. Some rooms offer splendid ocean views. Winthrop Arms has earned many accolades and has been featured on some of Boston's best travel and food programs, including WCVB's *Chronicle* and the *Phantom Gourmet*. Winthrop Arms is located in a residential neighborhood at 130 Grovers Avenue in Winthrop.

Regina Pizzeria

1926

For many folks, pizza in Boston is equated with only one long-standing establishment: Regina Pizzeria. Also known as Pizzeria Regina, this has blossomed into a mini-chain throughout New England, but the original is at 11½ Thacher Street in the North End. It has the feel of an old-school neighborhood pizza joint, with pictures of celebrity patrons on the wall and booth and table seating. Ever popular, this spot is known to have a line out the door. It's a perfect spot to grab a pie and a pitcher of beer.

Regina Pizzeria was established by Luigi D'Auria in 1926, with his grandson selling the business to the Polcari family in 1956. The Polcaris have owned the restaurant ever since and have expanded it to its current state. The pizza is known for its thin, crispy but chewy texture using the fresh ingredients of cheese, sauce, dough and various toppings. What makes the North End location so special, in addition to the atmosphere and the pizza, is the oven the pizza is baked in. The oven dates back to 1888. It was originally run on coal but was transferred to gas in the 1930s.

Most of the satellites of Regina Pizzeria are takeout spots in malls and other quick spots. The Allston location, however, took over the former Sports Depot building. (Before that, it was a train station built in 1887 by the famed architect firm of Shepley, Rutan and Coolidge, successors to Henry Hobson Richardson.) The Allston location also had the booths and tables like the original but was festively decorated in a celebratory fashion. This branch closed in 2020.

Regina Pizzeria is often voted best pizza in the city. *Jaclyn Lamothe.*

Regina Pizzeria has recently earned the accolade as the best pizza in the country, as ranked on TripAdvisor, and has been featured on the *Today Show.* Its slogan is "Welcome to Boston's Original Pizzeria." It is so associated with the city that it has been dubbed the "Official Pizza of the Boston Red Sox," having established a strong connection with the hometown team. In addition to the branches of the pizza restaurant, the Polcari family also run two Italian restaurants, both called Polcari's, with a full-service menu featuring favorites such as pasta, poultry and seafood dishes. Both of these are located north of Boston, in Saugus and Woburn.

For the authentic Regina Pizzeria experience, make sure to visit the original North End location. You won't be disappointed!

Charlie's Sandwich Shoppe

1927

Talk about a restaurant with a story to tell! Charlie's Sandwich Shoppe, located at 429 Columbus Avenue in Boston's South End, sure does. Charlie's is a small restaurant that is reminiscent of a diner or coffee shop and is a true old-school establishment. It specializes in breakfasts such as griddle cakes and eggs and lunch food such as burgers but is especially known for the turkey hash. Charlie's began way back in 1927 by Charlie Poulos. Other than its food, Charlie's backstory made it famous. For many decades, the eatery was open twenty-four hours a day, 365 days a year, including Christmas and Thanksgiving. Another distinctive feature was the lack of a bathroom (there is one today). Charlie's was also a hangout for African American jazz musicians who were staying nearby while playing in Boston. They would not be allowed service at segregated hotels, so for a late-night bite, they would venture over to Charlie's. Given the fact that Charlie's served African Americans when other area restaurants did not, it became a popular restaurant for the African American community of the South End. Above Charlie's was the location of the union hall of the Brotherhood of Sleeping Car Porters, the first African American union, founded by A. Phillip Randolph in 1925. Sammy Davis Jr. and Duke Ellington are some of the most famous musicians to be customers at Charlie's. The most famous customer in more recent times is President Barack Obama.

After Charlie Poulos's ownership of Charlie's, it was bought by the Manjourides family. After many years at the helm, they retired in 2014. It was reopened soon after by chef Evan Deluty and then sold to Damian and Sheree Marciante in 2017. They also own another classic Boston restaurant, Victoria's Diner, located at 1024 Massachusetts Avenue, which has been there since 1949 and serves traditional diner fare.

Hood Milk Bottle

1933

A long with Fenway Park, the Prudential Center and the Zakim Bridge, the Hood Milk Bottle, which is located outside of Boston's Children's Museum in the Fort Point neighborhood, is among the most iconic sites of modern Boston. Excluding historic structures such as the Bunker Hill Monument, the Massachusetts State House or Faneuil Hall, the Hood Milk Bottle ranks among the most recognizable structures in the city. Unlike most traditional classic Boston restaurants, the Hood Milk Bottle is a snack bar, without interior sit-down service. It would be remiss, though, to not include it in this collection.

Hood, along with other iconic Massachusetts brands past and present, including Friendly's, NECCO and Ken's Dressing, is simply part of the fabric of New England. In addition to the Hood brand being one of the most historic in Massachusetts, the milk bottle itself has quite a backstory. Hood Dairy, which is known for its milk, ice cream and sour cream, among other items, began in 1846 in Charlestown. The company has expanded tremendously since its inception over 170 years ago. It has acquired other brands under its banner, with its scope having expanded from solely a New England product to a national product. What has not changed is Hood's commitment to the region. It is still considered a local brand with its headquarters just a bit farther up Route 1 in Lynnfield, Massachusetts. The red-and-white oval logo is well known, as its imprint on dairy products is found in most refrigerators and freezers. The Hood blimp is even known to make appearances hovering above Fenway Park on game day.

The Hood Milk Bottle is a Boston landmark. *Author's photo.*

The HP Hood company (the official name, after the original owner, Harvey Perley Hood) has quite a history in itself, but the focus here is the Hood Milk Bottle. Located on the banks of the Fort Point Channel, rising over the bridge that connects downtown Boston to the Fort Point region of South Boston, is the milk bottle. This would seem more likely to be found among the roadside kitsch of Route 1 in Saugus, next to an orange dinosaur or a giant cactus road sign. Instead, this forty-foot-tall dairy vessel is smack dab in the middle of bustling Boston.

The milk bottle has graced the entryway of the Boston Children's Museum—which itself is a former warehouse for wool—since 1977. Actually, this neighborhood, which is now an entrance to the vibrant seaport district, was once teeming with warehouses, many of which were vacant, with the Children's Museum the only beacon among a sea of abandonment. Not so in the twenty-first century though, as the old meets the new in arguably Boston's hippest neighborhood.

Even though the fifteen-thousand-pound wooden milk bottle has watched over the canal and museum since 1977, the structure itself was erected decades earlier. In the city of Taunton, located in southeastern Massachusetts on Route 44, this milk bottle was built in 1933 (some sources say 1934) as an ice cream stand by Arthur Gagner for ice cream that he sold. Later, Gagner sold his ice cream stand to the Sankey family, who sold ice cream in the same location. By 1967, this stand was void of operation and was left as a roadside relic. In 1974, it was the subject of a famous photograph by Walker Evans, the photographer who was known for his iconic Depression-era pictures. The photo currently is the property of the Metropolitan Museum of Art in New York City.

As forlorn as the abandoned milk bottle appeared in Evans's famous 1974 photo, a year later, its fate was reversed. A clothing designer named Carol Scofield bought the abandoned structure for $2,500. Working with John Sloan, a director at the Boston Redevelopment Authority, on what to do with the structure, Sloan championed the idea of placing it in the newly redeveloped City Hall Plaza. It would be a place for cold treats in the summer and warm drinks in the winter and would liven up the drab brick and concrete plaza. Unfortunately, his idea was struck down by the mayor's office.

Through a connection, Hood footed the bill to rehabilitate the old milk bottle, although the location of it was in question. At this time, the Boston Children's Museum was in the process of moving from Jamaica Plain to the current location in Fort Point. The Children's Museum thought having the gigantic milk bottle—which, if filled with actual milk, could fit 58,620 gallons of it inside—was a grand idea. After being renovated, it was shipped from Quincy and placed on a barge that brought it to its current location. The pictures from April 20, 1977, are quite a sight—a forty-foot milk bottle winding its way around Boston Harbor in what became known as the "Great Bottle Sail."

Since 1977, the Hood Milk Bottle has achieved iconic Boston landmark status. It is officially located in Hood Milk Bottle Plaza, which is just outside the Boston Children's Museum. It's a fun entry into a child-pleasing location. Although there is no room for indoor dining, there are plenty of tables and chairs for eating outside. This once-dilapidated area of town is now a family favorite for both tourists and locals. The Harborwalk skirts all around the city's waterways, including next to the Fort Point Channel and Boston Harbor. The Hood Milk Bottle is a perfect stop-off for a snack or an ice cream while on this walk, even without entering the Children's Museum. Nearby is the Boston Tea Party ship and other classic Boston restaurants such as the Barking Crab and James Hook Lobster Company. In recent years, due to the elements, the milk bottle has been significantly repaired to help keep it a Boston landmark for years to come. In 2006, the top half of the bottle was taken off and the bottom half of the structure was replaced. It was moved to its current placement in what is now known as Hood Milk Bottle Plaza. On April 20, 2007, the restoration was complete, and the milk bottle was rededicated on the thirtieth anniversary of the Great Bottle Sail, the day it arrived at Museum Wharf (now called Children's Wharf).

The actual tenants of the milk bottle have changed over the years, among them local restaurant Sullivan's on Castle Island and the Boston area–based chain Au Bon Pain. Of course, Hood itself has also been a tenant. No matter who is serving, expect quick dishes such as hot dogs, sandwiches and, as always, ice cream.

Katz Bagel Bakery

1938

Tucked away in a neighborhood in working-class Chelsea, just over the river from Boston, is the purveyor of the area's finest bagels, Katz Bagel Bakery. This institution has been situated at 139 Park Street at the corner of Congress Avenue since it was opened by Harry Katz in 1938. In addition to the bakery's bagel fame, Katz's is also said to be the inventor of the pizza bagel.

Katz Bagel Bakery (which is actually pronounced *Kates*) is known for its bagels, pizza bagels and bagel dogs but also bagel chips, bread and cookies, as well as its frozen pizza bagels. The bakery was started by Harry Katz, a Russian Jewish immigrant. Bagels reached the United States via Eastern Europe from Jewish immigrants beginning in the late nineteenth century. Bagels became popular in New York City and soon spread to other East Coast cities. Chelsea used to be a Jewish neighborhood but in more recent years has become a popular city for other newly arrived immigrant groups. The storefront of Katz was a bakery before it was sold to Harry. Harry learned the bagel-making art from his uncle. At first, the bakery's focus was challah, bread, rolls and bagels, but it soon shifted to mainly bagels after the customers' reactions. Harry made each bagel by hand. When the process became mechanized, he was not happy with the machines that were on the market, so he created his own.

Son Richard Katz took over the business from his late father. Richard has worked in one way or another at the bakery since he was five years old. The

Katz Bagel Bakery, home of the pizza bagel. *Author's photo.*

family used to live in a small apartment over the bakery. The bakery is now in its third generation of Katz family since Richard's sons Jimmy and Jeremy help run the business. Katz is a small bakery with no seating inside. It is perfect for picking up bagels for breakfast, a sandwich for lunch or a pizza bagel for dinner. Throughout its history, only the freshest ingredients are used at Katz, nothing artificial. They are the perfect bagel. An ideal size—not too big, not too small. They are crispy on the outside and chewy on the inside, just what a bagel should taste like.

The most popular flavor is plain. One flavor that is unique to Katz is the onion bagel where the onion is mixed into the dough. It's called the onion inside bagel. They also serve a traditional onion outside bagel. Make sure to try the cream cheese too; the chive is one of the most popular. Pizza bagels make up about 50 percent of the sales at Katz. Interestingly enough, these are not just bagels with sauce and cheese on them. Instead, they are made with the bagel dough, not bagels themselves. The pizza bagel is an ideal combination of pizza sauce and cheese on the signature doughy bagels, which are soft and chewy. Another popular menu item is the bagel dog, a Chicago hot dog surrounded by delicious dough.

When Katz is asked about his product, he replies, "It's not rocket science," although the recipes are kept as a family secret. His bagel baking prowess helped launch the first successful bagel enterprise in China. In 1996, Mrs. Shanen's Bagels was opened in China by a Chinese American woman from Brooklyn. She was taught the bagel-making process by Katz, who also helped advise her throughout the process of starting her own bakery.

With Katz Bagel Bakery's reputation of making the best bagels in Boston for over eighty years, it has become a staple of the Boston "must list," visited by tourists from all over the world. Numerous accolades have been won by Katz in publications such as the *Improper Bostonian* as best bagel. Katz even sold its frozen bagels at grocery stores but has since ceased production. They are still able to be purchased at the store though.

For a true taste of Boston's best bagels, make sure to head on over to Chelsea. A trip to Katz Bagel Bakery is mandatory. Whether for a bagel, a pizza bagel or a bagel dog, you will not be disappointed. The shop is tiny, fitting just a few customers at once. On the weekends, don't be surprised to see a line out the door. The interior is completely old school. It's a no-frills bagel bakery. Look for the funny slogans too, such as "Buy Katz bagels, we knead the dough."

Legal Sea Foods

1950

Think about this. If in New England seafood is king, Boston represents New England and, to many, Legal Sea Foods is the epitome of Boston seafood, then this puts Legal Sea Foods at the top of the food chain in New England.

No matter how you slice it, Legal Sea Foods is an institution. Although it has outposts outside the Boston area, such as in Philadelphia and Washington, D.C., this is a Boston restaurant. Although there are currently over thirty restaurants in the Legal family (don't say chain!), it is associated with its hometown of Boston.

The restaurant is so ingrained in the fabric of our culture that hardly anyone stops to think why the name "Legal." Although the beginnings of the Legal fish market go back to 1950, the story dates back forty-six years earlier, from 1904. A man named Harry Berkowitz established the Legal Cash Market in Inman Square in Cambridge that year. The moniker of "legal" derives from the fact that the store took government-issued, legal stamps. The loyalty stamps were used by customers at the store, kind of like today's coupons or frequent buyer cards. Similar stamps were used in different large grocery stores as a customer loyalty program. Legal Cash Market was a local store, selling produce, meats and other groceries. Eventually, in the 1940s, the market started selling fish.

In 1950, Harry's son, George Berkowitz, opened Legal Sea Foods, an adjacent fish market to the grocery store, and ran it with his wife, Harriet. It was a fish market known for selling the freshest fish, something that Legal

Sea Foods still prides itself on today. As its motto reads, "If it isn't fresh, it isn't Legal." In addition to fish, shrimp, scallops and the like, the market also sold fish and chips to go. In 1968, Berkowitz annexed his father's grocery store as a restaurant. Known for its communal-style tables, it was a family-style establishment where the seafood was served either fried or broiled. Instead of waiting to bring all orders to the table at the same time, servers would bring the dish to the individual diner the second it was ready—again, freshness was key.

With the fish served at both the restaurant and the store, the reputation that Legal Sea Foods carried the freshest fish in town continued to grow. With ties to the Boston docks, Legal always served fish from the top of the pile, even when it cost more money to do so. Advocating for the freshest seafood is still a top priority at Legal Sea Foods, where they utilize an extensive quality control program. A champion of Legal Sea Foods was fellow Cambridge resident and world-renowned chef Julia Child. She was a frequent customer at the market.

With the success and reputation of the Inman Square restaurant, Legal Sea Foods opened a sister location in suburban Chestnut Hill in 1975. Unfortunately, tragedy struck five years later when the Inman Square restaurant was lost to history by a devastating fire. Legal relocated its flagship restaurant inside the Park Plaza Hotel in downtown Boston. This branch closed in 2020.

George Berkowitz's son and Harry's grandson, Roger, was named CEO of Legal Sea Foods in 1992. Under his guidance, the brand has continued its commitment to fresh and tasty fish but has expanded into other forays such as different concept restaurants and revised menu items. Roger Berkowitz had worked at his father's store since he was ten years old in some capacity. Returning from college at Syracuse in 1974 with a degree in journalism, with intentions of pursuing a career in this field, his dad asked if he could manage the Inman restaurant. He never left. Roger and brother Marc were put in charge of managing the flagship location at the Park Plaza. Roger Berkowitz sold the Legal Sea Foods restaurants to the PPX Hospitality Group in late 2020.

Legal Sea Foods also runs a quality control center in South Boston. Located here is a fish-processing plant and food safety laboratory. Just as always, Legal makes sure the fish is from the "top of the heap." This is important because the last fish caught in the day's haul lands on the top. The fish are studied and processed at this facility to make sure they are up to Legal Sea Foods' standards. This is nothing new for the company.

The government asked Legal Sea Foods to partner in creating the Hazard Analysis Critical Control Point (HACCP) along with the Food and Drug Administration, which is a seafood inspection program. Seafood is finicky, given polluted waters, microbes and toxins that can permeate the fish and thus infect the human consumer. It is extremely important to monitor the fish quality since eating fish can be unsafe, especially in dealing with popular menu items such as raw oysters and littlenecks.

Other initiatives with Legal Sea Foods at the forefront include removing trans fats from its food in the early 2000s. In 2005, long before it was chic or in the consciousness of the average consumer, Legal Sea Foods made a concerted effort to put gluten-free items on its menu in awareness of celiac disease.

In addition to numerous Legal Sea Foods restaurants, there are other varieties of restaurants under the Legal banner. These include Legal C Bar, Legal Harborside, Legal Crossing and Legal on the Mystic, as well as many outposts at Boston's Logan Airport and Ronald Reagan Airport. Former restaurants also included the Legal Test Kitchen and Legal Fish Bowl. Currently, there are over twenty restaurants under the umbrella, and further expansion to more airports is in the plans. Each of the different variations of Legal Sea Foods has a different angle. For example, the mixed drinks are a focus at Legal C Bar. Each has its unique spin but offers the same mouth-wateringly delicious seafood choices that have made the restaurant famous.

Currently, Legal Harborside is the flagship of the brand. It covers three floors, each with a different theme, with a casual chowder and oyster bar vibe downstairs, a formal dining room on the second floor and a chic bar and deck with spectacular views on the third floor. The name Legal Harborside represents much more than the fact that it is on the harbor in the heart of the ultra-popular Seaport District. The name is an homage to longtime classic Boston restaurant Jimmy's Harborside, a contemporary of such favorites as No Name Restaurant and Anthony's Pier 4. Legal Harborside is in the location of the former Jimmy's Harborside. Visitors to the Seaport during the era of Jimmy's would be shocked to see the development and glitziness of this neighborhood today. Once strewn with semi-abandoned warehouses, this neighborhood is currently the epicenter of Boston's vibrant restaurant scene and is a nightlife destination. Across the street was the location of the Legal Test Kitchen.

The executive chef and vice president of Legal Sea Foods is Rich Vellante. He has been with the company since 1998 and began working at the Chestnut Hill location.

A fun fact about the chowder, in addition to the fact that it has numerous "best chowder" accolades, is that it has been featured on the menu at each presidential inauguration since Ronald Reagan's in 1981. It began during Reagan's inauguration as part of a "Taste of America" display where two food items from each state in the Union were included on the menu. It has been a mainstay ever since, although in 2017, it almost did not make the cut for the inauguration of Donald Trump. Unbeknownst to his staff that the Legal chowder is a regular at this event, it was added at the last minute. The Legal chowder is known for its simple but delicious recipe. It is made in the New England style, which means that the base is cream, with the addition of clams, herbs, potatoes and onions.

Today's Legal Sea Foods is as popular as ever. With over twenty restaurants, the Legal brand appeals to diners of all kinds. From the classic, sit-down restaurants of Legal Sea Foods to the hip Legal C Bar and the numerous airport locations, the eateries run the full gamut of options. They serve over forty varieties of fish and shellfish. Whether you're in the mood for cod, a lobster or just a bowl of chowder, Legal Sea Foods delivers on all levels. One of the most popular dishes, as it has been for years, is Anna's Baked Scrod. Scrod is a Boston favorite. The fish is actually cod or halibut; there is no actual species of "scrod." The determining factor on what makes it scrod is its weight. It has to be less than two and a half pounds. Anna's Baked Scrod is the recipe of Anna McAllister, who was the first manager at Legal Sea Foods. She was from Ireland, and this recipe comes from her home. The scrod is topped with breadcrumbs and a tomato—a welcome change from all the fried seafood the restaurant was serving at that time. It's on the menu today as Anna's Baked Boston Cod. The Jasmine Special is also popular: shrimp on a bed of jasmine rice with cheese, served with broccoli.

For seafood lovers, a meal at Legal Sea Foods is a must while visiting Boston. Of course, if you're local, you've certainly already eaten at a Legal restaurant.

Sullivan's

1951

Depending on whom you talk to, South Boston, better known as "Southie," has two very different reputations. For the older generation, Whitey Bulger, the Winter Hill Gang and a racially fueled busing controversy in the 1970s come to mind. To the younger generation, Southie has become a gentrified upscale neighborhood with ocean views, full of fine dining and boutiques. One classic restaurant that comes to mind when thinking of Southie is Sullivan's at Castle Island.

Let's set a few things straight about the location. Any local will undoubtedly know that Castle Island is not actually an island, but presumably, most outsiders would venture to guess that Castle Island would require a boat of some sort (or maybe a long bridge) in order to set foot on it. Massachusetts does this to outsiders—for instance, dropping route signs in the middle of an intersection to let drivers guess that they are still on the correct road.

In actuality, Castle Island is a twenty-two-acre state park best known as the location of Fort Independence. Even though Sullivan's has been grilling up grub on Castle Island since 1951, this hardly compares with the longevity of the fort. The current stone structure was built in 1851, but this location has been fortified since 1634, making it the oldest such place in America that has been in continuous use as a fort. Although the fort is not used for defense today, it has become a tourist attraction in its own right. The fort never actually saw military action, but it did inspire a former soldier. Edgar Allan Poe was stationed at the fort and was inspired by a legend about a lieutenant, Robert F. Massie, who was killed in a duel after an argument. The legend

Sullivan's at Castle Island. *Jaclyn Lamothe.*

relates that Massie's friends coaxed the killer, Gustavus Drane, into a state of inebriation and then suffocated him by walling him up into a vault in the fort, thus inspiring the Poe classic *The Cask of Amontillado.*

Castle Island is a popular recreation area for Boston residents and visitors alike. There is a beach for swimming, a playground, many routes for walking and parkland for picnicking. The most popular route is the walkway around the perimeter of the fort. Another popular route is a walkway into the sea that leads back to William J. Day Boulevard.

Sullivan's is a beefed-up takeout stand that is located near the entrance to Castle Island, just past the parking lot. The parking lot has over two hundred spots but in season can fill up. Sullivan's address is 2080 William J. Day Boulevard. If parking is limited at Castle Island itself, the shore side of the boulevard is one long beachside promenade with parking alongside it. Unlike most addresses in Boston, parking here is free and typically plentiful.

The original Sullivan's takeout stand was opened in 1951 by Dan Sullivan Sr. Serving quick and easy items like hot dogs, burgers and ice cream, Sullivan's soon became a hit with locals. Twelve years later in 1963, Sullivan's was rebuilt into a more permanent structure. In 1986, the present brick building was erected. One neat historical tidbit is that the restaurant is actually patterned after the circa 1807 captain's quarters that was located there.

Sullivan's is something between a takeout stand and a restaurant. Customers line up inside the brick façade to order their meal. There are no waitstaff or tables inside. Instead, it is grab and go. In addition to your car, there are plenty of other seating options. Just outside Sullivan's is a collection of picnic tables. Plus, there are ample benches, beachside seating or seating in the grass.

The food at Sullivan's is not fancy, but it sure is good. The adage they swear by is "quality food at reasonable prices." This slogan is as relevant today as it was sixty years ago. The menu may be surprising though. Sullivan's is most famous for its hot dogs. What makes the pork and beef steamed dogs so delicious beats me, but I swear they are truly fantastic. These snap when bitten into. I typically opt for a slew of toppings, such as mustard, relish and onions or maybe even make it a chili dog. The hot dog itself though, even plain, is so good.

Sullivan's is also well known for its seafood selection. The variety of fried seafood includes clams—both whole bellies and strips—shrimp and fish. The lobster roll is a sight to behold. Extremely reasonably priced at less than $17.00, it is full of fresh meat, served on a buttered, toasted bun. It's a deal! All the prices are more than reasonable though. The whole belly clam platter is $22.00, and the hot dogs are $2.60 apiece. Nothing costs $2.60 these days! Other favorite menu items include burgers, featuring a double cheeseburger, crinkle-cut french fries, chili and onion rings. For dessert, it's ice cream. Another Sullivan's favorite is the raspberry lime rickey. This is a classic New England summertime sipper. It's simply seltzer, raspberry syrup and lime. Truly refreshing.

Hot dogs are a favorite menu item at Sullivan's. *Author's photo.*

Sullivan's has withstood the test of time, with the current owners, Branden and Adrian Sullivan, as the fourth generation to be at the helm. For almost sixty years, they have been grilling dogs and serving fresh seafood since way before South Boston became what it is today.

Celebrities such as Mark Wahlberg and Jack Nicholson are among the restaurant's more famous clientele. Sullivan's is only open seasonally, from February to November. I often frequent Sullivan's in the cooler months when the crowd is thin, even if it means eating in the car with the heat on. Even if the lines are long in season, they do move fast. Come to Sullivan's for delicious food and ocean views, and while you're there, spend a while exploring historic Castle Island.

Mr. Bartley's Gourmet Burgers

1960

M r. Bartley's Gourmet Burgers, also called Mr. Bartley's Burger Cottage, correctly labels itself as a "Harvard Landmark" on its sign. It has been situated in the heart of Harvard Square since 1960; much has changed in the square during that time, but Mr. Bartley's has not. In Bartley's sixty years, it has witnessed Harvard Square transform from bohemian to upscale. Personally, I've been coming to Bartley's since the 1980s. The burger names have changed and the decor has been expanded, but the vibe is exactly the same and the burgers are just as amazing.

Joe and Joan Bartley purchased the Harvard Spa in 1960. In the metro Boston area, a spa doesn't always mean a rejuvenating health club. For some reason, neighborhood convenience stores also take on the name "spa" in Brighton, Cambridge, Waltham and Watertown. There are many of these, including the Moody Spa in Waltham and Victoria Spa in Watertown. When Bartley's first opened, it sold items such as newspapers and cards but also added a grill where Joe Bartley wanted to serve the best burger possible. The most popular item at the store during the early days was the newspapers.

Sixty years later, the reputation is as strong as when it first opened. It's a fun and funky place with truly delicious burgers. Bartley's distinctive decor is similar to that of a dorm room. Think a slew of posters, sports memorabilia, bumper stickers and even MBTA subway signs hanging on the walls. The burgers have catchy names and are ever-changing. For instance, the Tom Brady burger (which has been on the menu for a while) will most likely be replaced since his departure from New England.

You know you're in for a treat at Bartley's! *Author's photo.*

Currently, other topical names for the burgers include Admissions Scandal, Julian Edelman and those of many local politicians, including Martha Coakley and Secretary of State William Galvin. Bartley's doesn't shy away from demonstrating its political leanings with the Trump Tower burger. In parenthesis on the menu it reads "new Russian Embassy." The burger mainstay has been lauded by such food shows as *Guy Fieri's Diners, Drive-Ins and Dives*, and the restaurant has a burger dedicated to him. Many of the burger names do change though. For instance, I distinctly remember eating the George Bush Jr. burger about fifteen years ago. For the Bernie burger, jalapeños can be added to "Feel the Bern."

Not only do celebrities show up in the burger names and through the memorabilia on the wall (including the Elvis Presley corner), but they have sat in the seats as well and eaten these unforgettable burgers. Among the most famous are Joan Baez, Shaquille O'Neal (whose Celtics jersey is in a case on the wall), Al Pacino (a plaque shows where he sat), Adam Sandler and Johnny Cash.

The burgers themselves begin with a juicy seven-ounce patty that current proprietor Bill Bartley grills himself. The Bartleys are into their third generation of the family business. Bill is Joe and Joan's son. He comes up with the clever burgers and names, a tradition started by his father. Joe passed away at the age of eighty-seven in 2018, but his wife can still be seen greeting the crowds at the restaurant. At Bartley's, expect some tongue-in-cheek, bawdy humor with burger names such as the Viagra. This burger is jam-packed with blue cheese, bacon, lettuce and tomato, and it "rises to the occasion." Another classic Bartley's line is the T-shirts with the slogan featuring a boxing burger: "You can't beat our meat." At the time of this writing, Bill is looking to sell but for Bartley's food and ambiance to remain, passing the torch on to a new owner.

Mr. Bartley's Gourmet Burgers is located at 1246 Massachusetts Avenue in Cambridge. Parking is difficult, with the T (the Red Line to Harvard Square) being the best bet. This is a very popular spot, at times with lines queued up outside. It's a snapshot of everyone who visits the Square. It's a hangout for Harvard professors, students, construction workers and tourists alike. As it always has been, Bartley's is closed on Sundays, is cash only and does not serve alcohol. In addition to the slew of burgers, Bartley's is known for its truly amazing shoestring onion rings dipped in a thin coat of batter, lime rickeys, frappes and sweet potato fries. A visit to Bartley's is a must when in Cambridge.

Cheers Beacon Hill

1969 (Originally Known as the Bull & Finch)

Arguably, the fame of Boston's most well-known restaurant is not due to its cuisine. Cheers, which was originally known as the Bull & Finch, saw its popularity skyrocket as it was broadcast into the homes of millions of television viewers from the years 1982 to 1993 on its namesake program, *Cheers*. Of course, the actual interior filming of the show took place on a Hollywood set, but the Bull & Finch served as the inspiration for its design, as well as being included in the actual exterior shots.

The establishment of the Bull & Finch occurred in 1969, but the impressive Georgian Revival building, known as the Hampshire House, that houses it dates from 1910 and was designed by Ogden Codman. With prime real estate at 84 Beacon Street, it is located on the north side of the Boston Public Garden. The former mansion is used as a function and event venue. It stands five stories in height, with Cheers in the basement.

Those who first step into this location of Cheers may be disappointed that it is not an exact replica of the TV show, or vice versa, that *Cheers* the TV show is not an exact replica of this place. There are many similarities though, including the faux-Tiffany hanging lamps, a wide bar and wood paneling. Don't forget about the scores of Boston sports memorabilia that both share. (An exact replica was located farther into downtown Boston at the Cheers Faneuil Hall location.)

The owner of the Cheers restaurants and the Hampshire House Corporation is Thomas A. Kershaw. In addition to Cheers, the group includes the restaurants 75 Chestnut, also in Beacon Hill, and 75 on Liberty

Cheers, the Bull & Finch, was the inspiration for the television show of the same name. *Ann Marie Lyons.*

Wharf in the Seaport District. Kershaw purchased the Hampshire House in 1969. At that time, the elegant Hampshire House building needed a bit of TLC. Ironically, before deciding on the purchase of the Hampshire House, Kershaw had the opportunity to acquire the Parker House Hotel, another famous Boston landmark.

Kershaw and his business partner, Jack Veasy, traveled to Bermuda that year. While in the city of Hamilton, they found their way into the Hog Penny, an English pub. This helped the duo decide on what to do with the basement of their building. They would turn it into an English-style pub. Looking for materials to purchase, they ended up having a team construct the bar in England and have the parts flown over to Boston, where they were then put together.

On December 1, 1969, the Bull & Finch Pub was open for business. The name is a nod to famed Boston architect Charles Bulfinch, who designed the Massachusetts State House located just up the road on Beacon Street. His other work includes the Old State House in Hartford, Connecticut, and the Harrison Gray Otis House, also in nearby Beacon Hill. Glen and Les Charles, writers of the *Cheers* television show, as well as director James Burrows, sought inspiration for their newly planned program. They settled on Boston and came across the pub. Visiting the Bull & Finch and talking with bartender Eddie Doyle, they found their inspiration in the basement watering hole in Beacon Hill.

With the fame of the television show, the Bull & Finch went from a neighborhood establishment known for its beers, burgers and Bloody Marys to a worldwide phenomenon. Regulars and locals found it hard to get a seat amid the throng of tourists. *Cheers* imprinted the Bull & Finch into the collective identity of the city of Boston. Boston in the twenty-first century is a tourist hub, a family-friendly city that is known for its world-class museums, tangible historical sites and popular sports teams. At one time though, Boston was not quite the destination it is today. Part of the resurgence of the city was through awareness due to *Cheers*. With Boston the tourist destination, a visit to the Bull & Finch was a must. Although the show was filmed in Hollywood, the Bull & Finch played host to the cast members at times, including a live broadcast of *The Tonight Show with Jay Leno* after the show's finale where the actors were clearly emotional and clearly intoxicated.

At the time of this writing, *Cheers* has been off the air for twenty-seven years. This has not caused Cheers the restaurant to lose any of its popularity. In 2002, after years of confusion that the Bull & Finch and Cheers were essentially one and the same, Kershaw had the name changed to Cheers

Beacon Hill, since the Faneuil Hall location had opened the year prior. Ever popular are the *Cheers* T-shirts and other souvenirs located in the gift shop. The menu at Cheers features classic dishes such as burgers, sandwiches, chowder and other pub grub. Menu items make reference to the show with "Norm's Sandwiches," "Sam's Starters" and "Woody's Garden Greens" among the food choice categories.

At Faneuil Hall, Cheers was located under a glass-enclosed portion of an exterior wing of the Quincy Market building. Unfortunately, this location closed in 2020. The interior of this establishment was a replica of the beloved bar from the TV show, albeit in a greenhouse-like surrounding. It included a large island bar where one would expect Sam "Mayday" Malone, Woody or Coach to be slinging beers. There was also outdoor seating available.

Longtime bartender and manager Eddie Doyle worked at Cheers from 1973 to 2009. His legacy is now commemorated with "Eddie Doyle Square" at the corner of Beacon and Brimmer Streets. In addition to being a Cheers mainstay, Doyle raised over $1 million for local charities such as the Jimmy Fund, which, along with the Red Sox partnership, raises money for the Dana-Farber Cancer Institute.

The next time you're looking for a place "where everybody knows your name," saddle up to the bar for a beer and a burger at Boston's Cheers restaurant. Dining here is a trip down memory lane for any fan of the show. And if you are not familiar with the television show, it is still a great place to grab a bite and a beer, as Norm would do on *Cheers*.

Cabot's Ice Cream and Restaurant

1969

The year man landed on the moon, the year of Woodstock, the dawning of *Sesame Street*—yes, 1969 was an important year. In the lore of Boston-area restaurants though, the opening of the widely acclaimed ice cream parlor Cabot's Ice Cream and Restaurant is equally as important. Cabot's is named for the surrounding neighborhood where the restaurant is located. Cabot is a popular place name in Newton, with Cabot Street and Cabot School close by. Newton comprises fourteen villages, and Cabot's is located in Newtonville on busy Washington Street, which parallels the Massachusetts Turnpike in what looks like an unassuming mid-twentieth-century commercial building. Step inside though, and you are transported into the ice cream parlor of your dreams.

The interior of Cabot's is bathed in black, white and red. The nostalgic black-and-white checkered floor is complemented by the red seats at the counter, booths and tables. The waitstaff's uniforms are also the classic white-and-red color scheme. Cabot's serves seventy flavors of homemade ice cream, with another thirty-five toppings that can be used to enrich your dish. Some of the more outrageous flavors include coffee Kahlua brownie, red velvet and Toll House cookie. Of course, more traditional flavors are also available. Cabot's is also known for massive party-sized ice cream creations. Take the $280 ice cream pyramid that feeds 175 people and includes sixty pints of ice cream. Even the biggest eater could not handle that food challenge! In addition to scoops of ice cream, Cabot's is known for its frappes, ice cream sundaes and floats.

If ice cream is not what is desired, never fear; Cabot's food menu is extensive and well-rounded. Breakfast is served all day. This is not just eggs and bacon though. Traditional waffles, omelettes and Belgian waffles are all on the menu, and so are hot cakes, which are super popular and unusual to see in New England. (Granted, they are essentially the same as pancakes, which are on many breakfast menus.) For lunch and dinner, Cabot's many options include salads, soups, sandwiches, burgers and classic American meals such as a turkey dinner. And the prices are very reasonable too.

It is hard not to have a smile on your face at Cabot's. With the friendly staff and the amazing ice cream and food, Cabot's is a winner. Cabot's also has a retro feel without being campy. Its vibe is from a bygone era, but the interior is spotless. It is basically the best of all worlds. Some diner-type restaurants may have a '50s feel but come off as tacky, and other old-timey places may look dingy. Not Cabot's. It combines the sheen of a brand-new restaurant with the friendly nostalgia of an ice cream parlor, a combination that is hard to come by these days.

Cabot's was started in 1969 by husband and wife Joseph and Catherine Prestejohn, who also previously ran Center Delicatessen in Arlington and Boulevard Restaurant in Allston. Cabot's is now operated by their children, Joseph and Susan, as well as their families. Cabot's is a strong supporter of community organizations, among them the local YMCA, area schools, the Rotary Club, the senior center and the Special Olympics. Cabot's is located at 743 Washington Street in the Newtonville village of Newton.

Harvest

1975

Harvest has been home to a veritable who's who of Boston celebrity chefs. So many alumni of this Harvard Square icon went on to own their own restaurants, become authors of cookbooks or both. Cambridge resident Julia Child even touted Harvest as one of her favorites. At Harvest, the farm-to-table concept was in vogue long before it became a nationwide trend. The cuisine is contemporary New England.

The restaurant is located down a circa 1969 alleyway between twentieth-century modern buildings that connects Mount Auburn Street to Brattle Street. Its small, unassuming neon sign has welcomed visitors to this just-off-the-beaten-path Cambridge stronghold for over forty-five years. Harvest has won accolades far and wide as a top Boston restaurant from publications such as *Travel + Leisure*, *The Improper Bostonian* and *Boston Magazine*.

The menu, though, is what has been drawing folks back to this hidden jewel for decades. The focus from the beginning, when the restaurant was owned by Boston-area restaurateurs Ben and Jane Thompson, was using the freshest ingredients to make exciting dishes not on the pages of most local menus. Today, the same philosophy still holds. Harvest was known to rotate its menu every two weeks, to grow its own herbs at the restaurant, to use vegetables from owner Jane Thompson's garden and to make its own bread and pasta, all at a time when olive oil as a dipping sauce for bread was considered extreme. At Harvest, these culinary practices popular today were a mainstay long before anyone else was doing them. During the 1970s, Harvest's bar was known to have a lively dating scene.

Harvest closed for a brief period in 1997, only to be opened a year later by Kenneth Himmel, a world-renowned real estate developer, who is also known for his other well-regarded Boston restaurants such as Grill 23, Bistro du Midi and Post 390.

Chef and author Sarah Moulton recalls working at the cold station, shucking oysters and clams while working at Harvest in the 1970s. Still on today's menu at Harvest are raw bar specialties. Harvest has also been known for its unusual game items offered, including boar, lamb and veal. It has even held wild game nights. In the same vein, Harvest's menu today contains dishes featuring venison. Diners enjoy Harvest's open, airy space; long, polished bar; and, in nice weather, a meal on the garden terrace. Harvest also has rooms available for private parties.

The résumé of former Harvest employees is mind-boggling. Some of the area's (and the nation's) best-known chefs honed their craft in this kitchen. These culinary heavyweights include chefs Frank McClelland, Barbara Lynch, Sarah Moulton, Chris Schlesinger, Jimmy Burke and Lydia Shire. Frank McClelland worked at Harvest from 1978 to 1981 as manager and eventually became executive chef. He would go on to open arguably the most highly regarded restaurant in Boston for many years, L'Espalier (now closed), as well as Sel de la Terre. Currently, he is the chef and owner of his namesake restaurant, Frank, in the town of Beverly on the North Shore of Massachusetts.

Chef Lynch is known for her extensive list of restaurants, including Menton, Drink, No. 9 Park, B&G Oysters, Sportello, Stir and the Butcher Shop, as CEO of the Barbara Lynch Collective. She is a James Beard "Best Chef of the Northeast" winner. Chef Moulton was the executive chef at *Gourmet* magazine, a Food Network personality and a cookbook author. Chef Schlesinger is best known as the proprietor of East Coast Grill, a long-standing restaurant in Cambridge's Inman Square, and also a James Beard "Best Chef of the Northeast" winner in 1996. Chef Burke opened such popular restaurants as Pembroke's Orta and Backyard Burger Bar in Scituate, both on the South Shore. Clearly, the list of Harvest alumni alone shows what an important gem this Harvard Square restaurant is.

As much as Harvest is built on its history of forward-thinking culinary skill and an extensive list of celebrity chefs who once graced its kitchen, it is as much on the forefront of Boston's restaurant scene under the leadership of Chef Tyler Kinnett as it was over forty years ago. Its menu focuses on the best local ingredients. Kinnett's past endeavors include Hamersley's Bistro, Fenway Park's prestigious EMC Club and Sel de la Terre. He has worked at Harvest since 2012, becoming executive chef three years later. Among his menu creations is the six-part tasting menu, which is a popular option at Harvest. From beef and chicken dishes to local seafood and interesting appetizers, Harvest remains a lunch and dinner destination. Couple that with a selection of local craft beers and handcrafted cocktails, and Harvest is a sure bet to satisfy even the most sophisticated palate. Harvest is located at 44 Brattle Street in Cambridge but is accessible through the walkway between Brattle and Mount Auburn Streets in Harvard Square.

SPOTLIGHT ON: LYDIA SHIRE

For over thirty-five years, Chef Lydia Shire has been bringing her culinary artistry to the kitchens of Boston. Shire was the first female executive chef in Boston when she helmed the kitchen at Seasons restaurant, which was located inside the Bostonian Hotel (now the Millennium Bostonian). Lydia Shire became owner and chef at Locke-Ober, an iconic French restaurant that dated from 1875, taking the helm of this Boston institution in 2001. Ironically, this dining establishment formerly did not allow women in its dining room. She also became chef in 1974 at the famous Maison Robert, a French restaurant located in Boston's Old City Hall. Her résumé also includes stints at the Four Seasons Beverly Hills and Pignoli in Boston. She was the owner of Biba and executive chef at Excelsior, both in Boston. She has opened Scampo and Towne Stove and Spirits (with friend and mentor chef Jasper White).

Scampo is located inside the Liberty Hotel at 215 Charles Street in Beacon Hill. The Liberty Hotel used to be the Charles Street Jail. Scampo is Chef Shire's take on rustic Italian cuisine. It opened in 2008 and ever since has earned numerous accolades, including being named one of the country's best new restaurants by *Esquire Magazine* in 2008. The food at Scampo not only includes Italian flavors but those of the Mediterranean and the Middle East as well. Among the chefs who have been mentored by Chef Shire are chefs Jody Adams and Gordon Hamersley.

Faneuil Hall Marketplace

1976 (Opened in Current Incarnation)

Faneuil Hall Marketplace consists of several buildings. Faneuil Hall, also known as the "Cradle of Liberty," as it was the site of impassioned speeches by the likes of Samuel Adams and James Otis that helped spur a revolution, dates from 1742. Directly behind this is Quincy Market, which will be the focus for this book since it is centered on food. Also here are the North and South Markets, as well as the Marketplace Center, bringing up the rear of the complex.

Although Faneuil Hall Marketplace's history harkens way back to the mid-eighteenth century, the current incarnation of the marketplace dates from 1976, 150 years after the building's construction date. Since then, this has become the touristy shopping and eating mecca that is known worldwide today. So popular is Faneuil Hall Marketplace that its annual number of visitors has actually topped those attending Walt Disney World. It is a combination of food, shopping (from Boston-branded tchotchkes to high-end stores such as Polo and Uniqlo) and entertainment, with jugglers and magicians, musicians and break-dancers. In the bottom floor of the Faneuil Hall building is an array of shops and vendors, while upstairs is found the Ancient and Honorable Artillery Company Museum, which is a military museum and library with artifacts showcasing America's military history. There is an emphasis on local though, with regional cuisine, outposts of Boston-area chains and New England stores such as Newbury Comics and the Black Dog with locations here.

Quincy Market is a bouillabaisse of different cuisines. *Jaclyn Lamothe.*

For the amateur gastronomist, the marketplace is a mélange of cuisines, types of eateries and price levels, thus the reason for its inclusion in this title. Entering through the Greek Revival columned front of the Quincy Market building (with its gilded lettering overhead), one walks into the Colonnade. The Colonnade is a long hallway with vendors ranging from almost any cuisine thinkable waiting for you to try their fare. In the middle, beneath the dome of the building, is the rotunda. Here is the scarce seating for the market. On a nice day though, many customers opt to nosh their selections out of doors in one of the many seating options.

Cuisine choices range from sushi and enchiladas to chocolate chip cookies and hot dogs. As this is a tourist hot spot, there are plenty of options for typical Boston fare, including New England clam chowder, oysters, lobster rolls and even Boston cream pie. One Colonnade vendor is Walrus and Carpenter (named for the Lewis Carroll poem in *Through the Looking Glass*), which has been shucking away at oysters since the inception of the remodeled market in 1976. In addition to the food Colonnade, there are a slew of other dining options located in the marketplace. Sit-down restaurants, such as Anthem, Wagamama, Ned Devine's Irish Pub and Mija Cantina and Tequila Bar, are also here for your dining pleasure. An outpost of Regina Pizzeria is also located here. A popular fish joint is the Salty Dog Oyster Bar and Grill. (We'll dive into this in the following section.) The restaurants are located all around the complex, from some in glass enclosures connected to the Quincy Market building to others in nearby South or North Markets, such as Mezcala Tex Mex Grill. Ned Devine's has the most interesting location; it's on the second floor of the Quincy Market building. Underneath the building is a variety of shops, as well as pushcarts, selling a variety of wares beneath an awning protruding from the sides.

Merchant Peter Faneuil donated the funds to establish a market, which was named after him, erected in 1742. After a fire in 1761, it was rebuilt completely. On top of the building is a Boston landmark, the gold grasshopper weathervane, which was said to bring good luck. Its history was tied in closely with that of the city. As previously mentioned, rabble-rousing orations by the likes of Samuel Adams and James Otis took place here, but it was also where the Committees of Correspondence were established. Faneuil Hall was used as a market but also as a town hall. At one such meeting in 1772, it was decided that correspondence would take place between Boston and other towns in the Commonwealth regarding their revolutionary ideas. In 1806, a third floor was added, designed by Charles Bulfinch. In the following decade, this was the location of speeches by abolitionists. In the twentieth century, the most famous Boston politician of the century, John F. Kennedy, spoke here.

Faneuil Hall's location as a market needed to be expanded, so thus was created what would eventually take the name of the building's catalyst, Josiah Quincy III, the second mayor of Boston. At this time, the harbor's water lapped just past the back door of Faneuil Hall, so the market had to be created on landfill, similar to a large portion of Boston. It was erected between the years 1824 and 1826, with Quincy laying the cornerstone. The primary architect was Alexander Parris, well known for other Boston-area landmarks such as Cathedral Church of St. Paul and the Church of the Presidents (final resting places of the Adams family).

Quincy Market's design is in the Greek Revival style, with a columned front and rear façade topped with a large central dome. The massive rectangular structure is 535 feet in length and built of Chelmsford granite culled from the Merrimack region of Massachusetts. It was used as an indoor market to buy groceries with an emphasis on produce and meat. Animals were slaughtered in the stockyards of Brighton to be sent over for sale at the market. It was also the home of the Boston Produce Exchange in 1877, and the Ames Plow Company held a warehouse on the second floor. Named for the company, the Ames Plow Tavern was a popular restaurant located at Quincy Market until 2015.

After a period of decline and neglect, the market reopened as a vision of a Boston tourism hub in 1976. Inspired by San Francisco's Ghirardelli Square, what became known as Faneuil Hall Marketplace became a focal point of the city. The success of Faneuil Hall Marketplace helped inspire other cities to revitalize similar areas, including Baltimore's Inner Harbor and New York City's South Street Seaport. The easternmost building in the complex, the Marketplace Center, was constructed in the 1980s. It is full of stores and used to block the unsightly Southeast Expressway (Interstate 93), which loomed above downtown Boston until it was routed underground with the Big Dig project completed in the early 2000s. Now, instead of covering an eyesore, it provides an archway to the beautiful Rose Kennedy Greenway, a chain of parks in the middle of Atlantic Avenue following the route of the former interstate.

THE SALTY DOG OYSTER BAR AND GRILL, 1972

One of the most popular eateries inside Faneuil Hall Marketplace actually dates from before the marketplace transformed into its current state. Located inside the Quincy Market but accessible from the outside concourse is the Salty Dog Oyster Bar and Grill. The Salty Dog is definitely a classic Boston restaurant. It serves all your favorite seafood. It's an urban fish shack offering lobster, New England clam chowder and fried clams. It has outdoor dining, a dining room and a bar.

The Salty Dog Oyster Bar and Grill actually predates the revitalization of Quincy Market. *Jaclyn Lamothe.*

TODAY'S FANEUIL HALL MARKETPLACE IS truly a centerpiece of Boston. With an immense variety of dining options, scores of stores and family-friendly entertainment, it has become one of the most visited places in the country. It will be crowded, and it certainly is not a hidden gem. Although other establishments may be a more authentic slice of the city, Faneuil Hall Marketplace and Quincy Market specifically make for a fun outing and should be on the itinerary for any visitor. Look for the many annual events that take place at the marketplace. One of the most popular is Blink, where the Faneuil Hall Marketplace is covered in holiday lights that blink in sync with seasonal music with a display every half hour.

The Barking Crab

1994

The Barking Crab, essentially a fish shack, sits on the Fort Point Channel and heralds itself as the gateway to the trendy Seaport District. Although this eatery is anything but fancy, it is still a very popular spot with locals and tourists alike. The Barking Crab opened its fresh-air location back in 1994, when the surrounding neighborhood was primarily vacant lots, copious parking lots and empty warehouses. Fast-forward to today, and the Seaport is the hot spot of Boston, with glitzy skyscrapers and expensive restaurants.

The menu at the Barking Crab is what one would expect for a fish shack in Boston—fried seafood, chowder, lobster rolls, crab options (hence the name) and cold beer. Originally, this was only a seasonal establishment, but the owners eventually purchased the Neptune Lobster and Seafood Market next to the restaurant, a building dating from 1886. With the use of a stove for heating in the winter, the Barking Crab is now a year-round seafood getaway. Harpoon beer is a specialty here. Harpoon Brewery is one of Boston's oldest, founded in 1986. It is located just down the road farther into the Seaport District.

Come to the Barking Crab for happy hour or on a weekend and expect a loud, boisterous crowd that is looking for a good time and great eats. The fun vibe is accented by communal picnic table seating. For its décor, think nautical with buoys, life rings and lobster traps bedecked in white lights. The restaurant is easy to spot with its red-and-yellow tent that covers the seating area. The large "Barking Crab" sign atop the restaurant is a sure giveaway. Even the building itself is robed in red.

The red and yellow awning marks the Barking Crab. *Author's photo*.

Whether you come for after-work beers or a fresh seafood dish, the Barking Crab will leave you satisfied. Most of the seafood is caught locally, and the lobsters are provided by James Hook and Company, a lobster mecca, located just across the Fort Point Channel in the Financial District. Current director of operations Alex Blake is steering the Barking Crab into its fourth decade. The Barking Crab is located at 88 Sleeper Street in Boston.

Anna's Taqueria

1995

Anna's Taqueria changed my life. I am not kidding. When I was a student at Boston University from 2001 to 2005, Anna's became my de facto dining hall for my junior and senior years. Prior to Anna's, the only Mexican cuisine I had tasted (and hated) was via chain restaurant Taco Bell just off the highway en route to my aunt's house in Pennsylvania. I found it bland, utterly tasteless. I'm not here to bash widespread Mexican restaurants. Instead, I'm here to champion the one, the only Anna's Taqueria.

My introduction to Anna's happened in 2002. I was living in an apartment-style dorm as a sophomore at BU. My roommates mentioned grabbing dinner at Anna's Taqueria, located nearby on Harvard Street in Brookline, only about a ten-minute walk from my dorm room at Packard's Corner in Allston. Back then, the restaurant had only four outposts, and the location at JFK Square in Brookline was half the size that it currently is. I walked in, stood in line behind my friends and first noticed the assembly line–like service of the restaurant. Meat? Rice, beans? Anything else? I answered the rapid-fire succession of questions as each ingredient was gobbed onto my open-faced burrito shell. I followed the lead of one of my roommates and opted for a super chicken burrito, which has been my go-to ever since.

Let's back up a bit to before that fateful day in the autumn of 2002. Even in 2002, a burrito was hard to come by in Beantown, especially one of extraordinary taste. Eighteen years later, Anna's is still the premier Boston burrito. (It has numerous accolades backing up this claim, not just by me.)

The truly amazing
burrito from
Anna's Taqueria.
Brian Samuels.

Anna's is a taqueria. This means food fast, not fast food. It's assembly line style. Rapid-fire ordering needs basic questions answered: What kind of meat? What kind of beans? And what extras: do you want guac, sour cream? Although dining in is an option, Anna's is not fine dining, no matter how you roll the burrito.

The inspiration for Anna's Taqueria harkens back to the Mission area of San Francisco, with the style of burrito they serve at Anna's being known as a "mission burrito." Anna's opened up in 1995 after a legendary dispute. Anna's owner, Michael Kamio, was employed as a manager of one of his sister's restaurants, Boca Grande, the first Tex-Mex establishment in Boston. Michael broke away, forming his own brand of Mexican delights in 1995. (More about the sibling rivalry later in this chapter.) According to Mary DiLeo, the public relations representative for Anna's, the name "Anna" was chosen because "the owners felt that the name evoked a familiar, maternal character whose kitchen is warm and inviting."

The menu at Anna's is not extensive: burritos, tacos, plates, salad bowls, that's about it. Wash it all down with a Jarritos Mexican soda or a fountain drink. What Anna's lacks in variety it makes up for in consistency and value. No doubt about it, you will walk away satiated, both in taste buds, stomach capacity and the size of your wallet after a meal at Anna's. Although the prices have risen over the years, the value is still tremendous. (For extrabig eaters, Anna's offers gigantic burritos, including the Cubio, a burrito that measures two and a half feet in length!) Today, Anna's has seven locations. The original, located in Coolidge Corner in Brookline (opened in 1995), closed in 2020. The second, and now oldest, location, mentioned above, opened in 1997 on Harvard Street in Brookline. This location is complemented by others in Porter Square, in Davis Square, at MIT, in Beacon Hill, in Newton Highlands and in the Prudential Center. Stopping into a satellite location, the grub is just as good as at the original Brookline spot. Even though the Anna's Taqueria on Harvard Street in Brookline doubled its size, the location with the claim to fame as the largest Anna's is the Newton Highlands restaurant.

The bestseller at Anna's Taqueria is the super chicken burrito. The super burrito is rolled in a twelve-inch tortilla, compared to the regular at ten inches. The cheese is steamed right into the flour tortilla, which makes up the backbone of each burrito at Anna's. From there, customers decide what they would like to fill it with. No matter what you choose, the ingredients are super fresh and always extremely flavorful. Distinctive in the salsa or pico de gallo at Anna's is the liberal use of cilantro. One fact that makes Anna's stand out from the pack in a day and age when a taqueria or other Mexican restaurant can be seen in almost every Boston neighborhood is that the burritos are perfectly rolled at Anna's. Even though Anna's prides itself on hearty, filled burritos, the key to their deliciousness is that each ingredient is

What to choose? *Brian Samuels.*

evenly dispersed inside the tortilla shell. This means that instead of one bite that is only rice, only bean or only guacamole, at Anna's, each bite presents a balance of all ingredients at one time. This makes Anna's a complete dining experience for lovers of burritos and other Mexican favorites. Don't just take my word for it, as the website Thrillist named Anna's Taqueria one of the best burritos in the country.

ANNA'S TAQUERIA VERSUS BOCA GRANDE: A SIBLING RIVALRY

Boca Grande is another tasty taqueria that has locations currently in Brookline and Cambridge. These days, its popularity is not quite on the same playing field as Anna's. Rewind thirty-odd years ago, though, for the whole story. Boca Grande was the brainchild of Bay Area resident Mariko Kamio. She moved from San Francisco to the Boston area and opened up Boca Grande in 1986 in the Porter Square section of Cambridge. At that time, Boca was the first Tex-Mex establishment in the Boston area.

Boca Grande was patterned after Gordo Taqueria in San Francisco. This highly successful California taqueria chain's proprietor was a cousin of Kamio. Mariko Kamio had established a lucrative and delicious business in Boca Grande, which had several other locations in the mini-chain. Her brother, Michael, was hired to manage some of these restaurants in the 1990s. Michael worked for Boca Grande for five years before opening his own restaurant, Anna's Taqueria, in 1995. Although Boca Grande was always a highly successful taqueria in the Boston area, its popularity began to wane, culminating with the retirement of its owner, Mariko, in 2016. Currently, there are two locations of Boca Grande: Brookline Village and Cambridge. When I was in college, it was a dispute among friends: Anna's versus Boca. At that time, Boca Grande had a location also in Coolidge Corner, only about three blocks or so from Anna's. Boca prided itself on a wider menu, with options such as a Colorado chicken burrito in addition to the regular chicken burrito. This rift continued toward the present day. Sadly, Michael Kamio, proprietor of Anna's for almost twenty-five years, passed away unexpectedly in 2019. Boca Grande is currently owned by Silvia Whitman, who was an employee for twenty-five years at the time of purchase in 2016. Both Anna's and Boca Grande are outstanding taquerias. I always opted for Anna's, but it was often a toss-up.

Zaftigs Delicatessen

1997

Although Zaftigs Delicatessen has only been in existence since 1997, it is one of those restaurants that clearly make up the fabric of a place. It's hard to imagine Coolidge Corner, a neighborhood in Brookline, without it. Zaftigs is a Jewish deli in a neighborhood that has many Jewish elements, including synagogues, delis and stores. Zaftigs is your quintessential neighborhood restaurant, offering breakfast (available all day), lunch and dinner in a fun and inviting atmosphere.

Zaftig, which the restaurant defines as a "plump Jewish mother," is represented by the deli's mascot of sorts, Nanny Fanny. She is pictured in the restaurant as a portrait by artist Danny O. According to the restaurant, she represents the ethos of Zaftigs: family, food and fun. According to the dictionary definition, *zaftig* means "having a full, rounded figure; plump." Both definitions are more than adequate to describe the character of Nanny Fanny. According to restaurant owner Robert Shuman, she embodies the Jewish mother, forcing another helping of food. She is always bedecked in her housecoat, and just like the matron of the family, she wants all of the family members together and eating.

At Zaftigs, expect the staples of a Jewish deli, including smoked fish plates, corned beef and pastrami sandwiches, latkes, matzo ball soup, brisket and even chopped liver. The bread choices go way beyond white and wheat to challah and marble rye. Although traditional Jewish deli fare is served here, it is a non-kosher restaurant. This means it serves a mean Reuben sandwich. In a kosher establishment, cheese and corned beef could not be stacked side by side. In addition to the traditional deli items, expect breakfast all day. Also, expect big portions. Dinner food includes kabobs, sandwiches and interesting spins on dishes, including the Latke Piccata, which is a lemon garlic chicken on top of a latke. Breakfast is served all day. Other menu items such as Reuben and Rachel sandwiches are available on the lunch and dinner menu. The New Yorker combines the best in the meat department: corned beef and pastrami.

Owner Robert Shuman grew up in a Jewish household in Boston. Recipes at Zaftigs come from his mom, Rubylee, and grandmother. Shuman's children also work for the restaurant. It is truly a family affair.

Food at Zaftigs is based on the tradition of Ashkenazi Jewish food and is a stalwart in the Jewish enclave of Coolidge Corner. The Jewish deli hit the shores of America through New York City. Many Jews immigrated to the Big Apple, eventually selling traditional foods via carts on the side of the road. In time, these carts became actual restaurants, and thus, the Jewish deli was born. In the twenty-first century though, especially in Boston, these are a rare commodity. Other Jewish restaurants in Brookline include Kupel's Bakery and Michael's Deli. Actually, the site of Zaftigs was once part of the Boston-area chain of New York–style delicatessens Barney Sheff's. With locations throughout the region, Sheff's was known for its corned beef sandwiches. Its flagship was located on Spring Street in Boston.

At Zaftigs, it is a common sight to see lines out the door waiting for a table, especially on the weekends. The most popular time for Zaftigs is between Rosh Hashanah, the Jewish New Year, and Yom Kippur. This period occurs during the fall. When you do get a table, make sure to nosh on the bagel chips and cream cheese, which are brought to the table gratis. The menu is huge; whether you opt for breakfast, a classic sandwich or a dinner entrée, it is hard to go wrong at Zaftigs. Zaftigs is located at 335 Harvard Avenue in Brookline, with a second location that opened in 2011 at 1298 Worcester Avenue in Natick (Route 9) in the Sherwood Plaza Shopping Center. Whatever you order, I can promise that you will not go home hungry.

Jasper White's Summer Shack

2000

Jasper White, along with fellow chef and good friend Lydia Shire, helped revolutionize the Boston restaurant scene in the 1980s. He opened his namesake restaurant, Jasper's, on the Boston waterfront in the early 1980s. After rave reviews and even recognition from James Beard, he closed it in 1995. The menu contained seafood options done in a creative way. Five years later, he surprised many Bostonians by opening Jasper White's Summer Shack in the Alewife section of Cambridge. The fact that White's restaurant featured seafood was not in question. What was surprising was that it is a New England clam shack, albeit an extremely large one with an extensive menu and top-notch taste.

Jasper White believes that the ingredients themselves are most important to taste. This is why fresh local fish is what is served at the Summer Shack. Summer Shack has maintained strong relationships with the fishermen and farmers who catch and grow what is cooked at the restaurant. At first glance into any of the three Summer Shack locations (Alewife, Back Bay or Mohegan Sun Casino in Uncasville, Connecticut), the customer notices the fun décor. It is reminiscent of a Cape Cod fish house on a much grander scale. There are images of fish and seafood that are larger than life. Bright colors and a fishy interior add to the fun.

The menu consists of what is expected from a seafood restaurant. With lobster, oysters, fried clams and chowder, seafood lovers are in their glory. With a chef with the expertise of White, expect wonderful meals. Among the most popular is the pan-roasted lobster. This dish alone has earned the

Food is love at Jasper White's Summer Shack. *Author's photo.*

restaurant accolades. The sauce, made with bourbon, chervil and chives, is simple and absolutely delicious. Lobster is cooked in many other ways too, including steamed, baked and stuffed, grilled or served on a lobster roll. Other rarer seafood delicacies such as king crab can be found here, although most of the seafood comes from the local waters of Cape Cod Bay. If seafood isn't your thing, the Summer Shack is known for its steak and, surprisingly, fried chicken. The oyster bar is stocked with a full selection of briny bivalves. Others stop by the Summer Shack for a tiki drink and a cup of chowder. For even more fun, there are fair food favorites, such as corn dogs, on the menu.

The slogan of the Summer Shack is "Food Is Love." Not only will you fall in love with menu items here, but the food is grown, caught and cooked with love. The phrase is in reference to the passion of the farmers and fishermen whose ingredients make the Summer Shack a beloved Boston restaurant. Local food writer Annie Copps voted the chowder here her favorite in Boston. The restaurant was nominated for a James Beard award in 2001 for Best New Restaurant.

At Jasper White's Summer Shack, it is summer all year long. The tasty seafood and the fun atmosphere are all part of the experience at the Summer

Shack, no matter which location you choose. With oysters, lobster and corn on the cob, the classic summer clambake is available all year round. The freshest ingredients speak for themselves as they take center stage on the menu at Jasper White's Summer Shack. The restaurant is a perfect intersection where a casual seafood shack meets big-city tastes. It has wowed crowds for over twenty years, making it a classic Boston restaurant.

SPOTLIGHT ON: JASPER WHITE

Although Jasper White was born in New Jersey, his culinary career is synonymous with the city of Boston. White prefers to champion the freshest of ingredients in his dishes, not a certain cooking style. He graduated from the Culinary Institute of America in New York, after which he spent time cooking in New York, Florida, California, Washington and even Montana. He relates that he learned his love of food from his grandmother.

White moved to Boston in 1979 and has been a fixture in the city ever since. He worked with fellow Boston chef extraordinaire Lydia Shire at such fine dining establishments as the Copley Plaza Hotel, the Parker House Restaurant and Seasons, inside the Bostonian Hotel. With Shire, he helped create an upscale American cuisine that flourished in the city. In 1983, he opened Jasper's on the Boston waterfront. With a menu focusing on seafood as well as other dishes, it earned rave reviews. Combining the freshest ingredients with sophisticated tastes, the restaurant thrived and put White on the culinary map. He earned the James Beard award for Best Chef of the Northeast. White closed Jasper's in 1995 due to the Big Dig, a massive construction project that lasted decades when all was said and done. One main goal of the Big Dig was to move the Central Artery (Interstate 93), which cut through the city, from a towering highway above Boston to be repositioned underground, with the intention of eliminating traffic problems and beautifying the skyline and streetscape. At that time, the highway created a barrier separating downtown Boston from the neighborhoods and areas to the east of the interstate. With Big Dig construction commencing, White did not want to have that interfere with his restaurant and closed its doors.

After Jasper's, he became a culinary consultant for Legal Sea Foods. He also became an established author, penning four cookbooks that include *Jasper White's Cooking from New England*, *Cooking Lobster at Home*, *Fifty Chowders* and *The Summer Shack Cookbook: The Complete Guide to Shore Food*. In 2000, he opened the first of his Summer Shack restaurants. It continued his tradition of shore food but cooked in a simpler way. This was a fish shack where customers could expect to get their hands dirty but still experience the vibe of a cool city spot. White is a lover of shore food and a lover of the freshest ingredients, as evidenced at his earlier restaurants. The traditions continue at Jasper White's Summer Shack.

PART III

NEIGHBORHOOD CLASSICS

The North End

T he North End is Boston's Italian neighborhood. Exploring this section of town feels as if you stepped back in time or overseas to Italy. The main streets and small alleys of the North End have a truly authentic feel. Expect to overhear conversations of locals spoken in the native tongue. Bocce, cappuccino and, of course, Italian food are further elements of the North End. The two main streets, Hanover and Salem, are lined with Italian eateries, many of which have graced the same storefronts for years. Restaurants such as L'Osteria, La Famiglia Giorgio's and Giacomo's have been here seemingly forever. True to its acclaim, it's hard to get a bad meal in this neighborhood. Once more of a hidden gem, especially when obscured by the Route 93 Central Artery expressway, North End restaurants are now popular dinnertime destinations for locals and tourists alike, meaning it is best to call ahead for reservations on weekends.

The North End is as close to mainland Europe as one can get in New England. During the summer, al fresco dining tables line the main thoroughfare, Hanover Street, as well as Salem and North Streets. People-watching accompanies a hearty Italian meal, just as it does in the old country. Walking down the street, you will hear Italian being spoken and see laundry hung out windows from clotheslines. The twisty back lanes of the North End are genuine. If you didn't know better, you'd swear you are in an urban neighborhood in Italy. In addition to the sights and sounds of Italy, smell is just as important, maybe even more so. Walking on roads

The North End is known for its Italian specialties. *Jaclyn Lamothe.*

such as Thacher Street and Salem Street, garlic literally wafts through the air. If you weren't hungry before, just stroll a bit in the North End and you soon will be.

In addition to delicious Italian dishes, other North End mainstays include the ever-popular Caffe Vittoria for cappuccino and other hot drinks. It has been around since 1929. In the pastry wars of the North End, bakeries vie for the title of best cannoli, with strong but friendly competition among Mike's Pastry, Modern Pastry and Bova's Bakery. In the summer, try to align your visit with a feast day celebration, featuring a festival, as well as a parade in the streets.

While this neighborhood is most closely associated with its Italian heritage, dig a little deeper and you will find traces of its former self. First and foremost, in North Square is located one of Boston's oldest homes, the Paul Revere House. Thought to be built around the year 1680, it stands out as a wooden home in a neighborhood dominated by brick façades. Other colonial traces of the neighborhood include the Christ Church in the City of Boston, better known by its more famous nickname, the

Old North Church. This was the site of the lanterns hung in the window during Paul Revere's (and others') famous midnight ride: "One if by land, two if by sea." These two stops, along with Copp's Hill Burying Ground, the second-oldest cemetery in the city, are on the Freedom Trail. Look for the tree-lined Paul Revere Mall just behind the Old North Church with an entrance on Hanover Street. It's a quiet oasis among the hustle and bustle of the neighborhood. The Freedom Trail connects the historic Boston sites of the Revolutionary War on a walking tour, a must for anyone visiting the city. Also in the cemetery are the unmarked graves of many African Americans, another group of people who inhabited this area of the city. The North End was also a primarily Jewish neighborhood and was then associated with the Irish before its current relationship with the Italian heritage.

In true Bostonian fashion, the streets are literally a maze of small corridors and alleyways supported by Commercial Street, Atlantic Avenue and Cross Street, with Hanover Street as the main thoroughfare through the neighborhood. Hanover is heaven for foodies, as from top to bottom it is full of spectacular dining options. Nearby North and Salem Streets also are known for their eateries. Don't discount the smaller streets though, as good grub and an Italian street scene can be found everywhere in this quaint enclave. For instance, the original Regina Pizzeria (previously mentioned in this book) is located on Thacher Street, one of those small North End hidden side streets.

Today's North End is a mix of the old generation and newer Boston residents, as this neighborhood, as almost all of the city, has become gentrified and pricey. With the completion of the Big Dig, the North End is linked by the beautiful Rose Kennedy Greenway, a chain of public parks that includes a beer garden, a carousel and food trucks in warmer months. Prior to that, the megalithic steel support of the Central Artery (Interstate 93) used to separate the neighborhood from nearby Government Center and Downtown Crossing. Now, the center of the city is a seamless patchwork of neighborhoods, of which the North End is fluidly part. For dining options, it is hard to go wrong here, but I have highlighted some of the most classic restaurants and eateries in the North End.

Note: Regina Pizzeria is also located in the North End. It is mentioned earlier in the book since it has outgrown its point of origin and has become a multi-restaurant chain. Granted, the original in the North End is the most authentic and is certainly a mainstay of the neighborhood.

CAFFE VITTORIA, 1929

Stepping inside Caffe Vittoria is truly like taking a step back in time. From its small round marble tables to its gleaming tin ceiling and antique metal cappuccino machines, you know you are someplace special. Dating from 1929, Caffe Vittoria prides itself on being the first Italian café in the city. This is no ordinary cappuccino bar. The establishment is spread across four floors. Its main dining room serves its famous hot drinks, including espresso, hot chocolate and cappuccino. Also served here are Italian specialties such as cannoli and tiramisu, as well as gelati. In the basement of the café is Stanza Dei Sigari, which translates to "cigar bar." The last of its kind in Boston, the interior is plush with dark woodwork and includes an extensive bar. Caffe Vittoria is located at 290–96 Hanover Street.

CANTINA ITALIANA, 1931

This North End mainstay bills itself as the "oldest restaurant in the North End." At about ninety years old, in terms of restaurants, this is ancient. Notice the large retro sign that adorns the façade of the restaurant, which is located at 346 Hanover Street. Part of the retro neon-lit sign's design is the wine bottle on top that drips into a glass below. The restaurant is known for its classic Italian dishes, such as spaghetti alle vongole, clams in oil and butter. It's a simple dish but is truly delicious. Another favorite is pollo e broccoli Americano, pan-seared chicken and broccoli over fusilli with an ample amount of cheese blended in. Pick from one of the many wines on the wine list. The interior includes a large bar close to the door and white tablecloth–covered tables, all of which evoke a classic Italian feel. During the warmer months, it is a fabulous place to relax outside and dine al fresco.

POLCARI'S COFFEE, 1932

The first visit to Polcari will promise to be a memorable one. Amble into this coffee, tea and Italian product shop on Salem Street and ogle at the counter. It has the feeling of an old-fashioned candy store. But instead of just candy (although it is also sold), there is a world of coffee, teas, spices and Italian specialties. The coffee shop was started by Italian immigrant

La Cantina Italiana, the oldest Italian restaurant in the North End. *Author's photo.*

Anthony Polcari. As a family affair, it was also run by his wife, Rose, and his children, Ralph, Anthony and Maria. Ralph would be the heir apparent to the business. Today, the store is owned by Bobby Eustace, who bought the business from Polcari before he passed away. After Polcari retired, he still would come into the store almost daily until his death in 2010. Eustace has continued to keep the Polcari tradition and timeless feel. He has been working at the store since 1984, when he was only seventeen years old, working for twenty-six years alongside Ralph Polcari. Ralph took over the store when his own father passed away the same year, in 1984. In addition to keeping up the store in the same feel as it always has, Eustace has continued the tradition of friendly service with a personal touch. Although the North End is often full of tourists, he greets everyone as if they are from here; granted, he also knows many regular customers by name. This is a lesson learned from Ralph Polcari, who seemed to know just what the customer wanted. Polcari never had kids, but six guys who worked for him, including Eustace, became like sons to him.

The store is very different from most city bodegas. It is reminiscent of a business found in the old country or, in a way, a general store, but certainly not a local Boston grocer. Instead of tablet card readers and computers, the mechanisms that control the flow of the business include scales for weighing coffee and tea that date from the early twentieth century, as well as an antique cash register. Items for sale line shelves in a unique way that is orderly but not rigid like at a chain grocery store or mini-mart. There are photos on the wall of the Polcaris of yore, along with a tribute to Boston sports. In addition to the coffee, tea, herbs, spices, nuts, pasta, candy and other items for sale, try the lemon slush. It is a refreshing frozen treat that is available in the summertime. Polcari's Coffee is located at 105 Salem Street.

GALLERIA UMBERTO, 1965

Galleria Umberto is a whole different experience from most dine-in North End Italian restaurants. This lunch-only establishment is where a cafeteria meets a deli counter. Looking for this hole-in-the-wall spot on Hanover Street, eyes are drawn initially to the old-school sign in black and white that reads "Galleria Umberto Rosticceria," with a Coca-Cola logo beneath it. If your visit falls between the hours of 10:45 a.m. and 2:30 p.m. on a Monday through Saturday, the next thing you will notice will be the long line extending from the counter often all the way to the street. (Just don't try to go during July, when the family takes the month off.)

The most popular menu item is the pizza. The sheet pizza is sold by the slice, and the rectangular, Sicilian-style slices are large. It's a perfect mix of dough and cheese, crispy without being burned. Some argue this is the best slice in town. Among the believers is *Zagat*, which ranked this the best pizza in

Boston. Co-owner Paul Dueterio and his family moved to Boston from Italy in 1958; Paul started working for his family as a kid. The family purchased a bakery on Parmenter Street in 1965 and eventually began selling pizza. This location, Galleria Umberto, was founded in 1974, with the original bakery closing in 1988. Today, Dueterio owns Umberto's with his brothers. The name is in reference to their father, Umberto Dueterio, and also to one of his father's favorite locations, Galleria Umberto, a grandiose shopping arcade in Naples.

The restaurant says it is open until 2:30 p.m. every day but often sells out before closing time. Prior to establishing the restaurant, the building was lodging for sailors spending time in port. At this location earlier were two churches, the New Brick Church and later a church that was severely damaged in a hurricane and had to be razed. Perched atop the roof of the first church was a weathervane of a golden rooster. The original is now part of a museum's collection. A replacement was stolen, but Paul Dueterio had a replica of the original piece made and put on top of the building. In addition to pizza, also popular at Galleria Umberto are their arancini, panini and panzerotti. The arancini here are legitimate; these fried delicacies are stuffed with rice, meat and peas and served with sauce. The panini are not pressed sandwiches but a tubular bread inlaid with Italian meats. The panzerotti is a potato and cheese concoction loaded into dough. The interior of the restaurant has wooden tables for two, with larger tables toward the back. The no-frills establishment offers plastic cups of red wine from the cooler. Order at the counter, but make sure to remember to bring cash. Galleria Umberto is located at 289 Hanover Street.

THE DAILY CATCH, 1973

Do you like calamari? If so, you must try the Daily Catch. With branches in Brookline; Woodstock, Vermont; and the Boston Waterfront, its original location is the cozy spot on Hanover Street. This small restaurant has been a North End staple since 1973. Founder Paul Freddura originally called his restaurant Calamari Café. After Paul met his wife, Maria, in 1979 and eventually had seven sons, the restaurant expanded into the Daily Catch that we know today.

Of course, all of the restaurants in the Daily Catch collective deliver delicious seafood and homemade pasta. Dining at the North End location, though, is special. First of all, the restaurant space is tiny. They do not take credit cards, and the primary ingredient on the menu is calamari. The homemade pasta is simply wonderful, and the black pasta is actually made with squid ink. Expect fried seafood options, as well as seafood over pasta. My favorite dish at the Daily Catch is the calamari platter. This features fried calamari, calamari salad and a calamari meatball; it is simply divine. This is an old-school, cash-only establishment. It is located at 323 Hanover Street.

L'OSTERIA, 1985

L'Osteria is a small Italian restaurant that exemplifies the true North End. The exterior's brick façade and awnings tempt passersby to come in for a meal in a place filled with old-world charm. Notice the intricacies of the building's architecture, including the upper floors, which house, presumably, apartments. It has such an authentic European feel. The interior's décor is simple but tasteful. There is nothing flashy about it, but come sunset, it is a perfect backdrop for a date night. The name *Osteria* in Italian refers to a simple place to eat. Some restaurants are more decorated with awards than L'Osteria, but remaining a viable establishment in the North End after more than thirty-five years, this place has to be doing something right. This has been a favorite of mine since I was a child. L'Osteria and Florence's Restaurant, which was located on North Street, right next to the Paul Revere House, were the two Italian eateries my family would go to after a day out in Boston. Still, my favorite meal on the menu after all these years is the linguini with mussels. Try it either with a tomato sauce or with garlic, oil and a white wine sauce. Of course, the menu is full of pasta choices and has a focus on seafood, veal and chicken dishes. The family-owned L'Osteria is located at 104 Salem Street.

LA FAMIGLIA GIORGIO, 1990

La Famiglia Giorgio is one of those restaurants that exemplify the North End, with a jovial atmosphere, a classic brick façade and immense portions. After your visit, you're certain to exclaim, "Mamma mia!" The staff of La Famiglia Giorgio treat customers like family—hence the name—and take pride that eating food in their restaurant is like being at Grandma's or, as they say in Italy, Nonna's. The cuisine is Roman, with heaping portions of pasta. Try the homemade take on tortellini, fusilli and rigatoni, among

L'Osteria, one of the many classic restaurants of the North End. *Jaclyn Lamothe.*

other pasta types. It is also known for the variety of delicious sauces for the pasta and extensive wine selection. Also on the menu are meat and fish dishes and, of course, pizza. For guests with dietary concerns, La Famiglia Giorgio is also known for its gluten-free options, a welcome sight in the old-school North End. The interior is dimly lit, with a mural, wine on display and a brick accent wall. For all you big eaters, make sure you inquire about the challenge plate. For instance, for fifty bucks you will be served six pounds of lasagna. Eat it all, and you will take home a T-shirt. There are many other choices of large quantities of food to consume. As far as accolades, the restaurant has been recognized in numerous publications, including *USA Today* and *Wine Spectator.* La Famiglia Giorgio is located at 112 Salem Street.

MONICA'S FAMILY OF RESTAURANTS, 1995

Within twenty-five years, the collection of Monica's restaurants has become a North End institution. These restaurants are owned and operated by the Mendoza family, Argentinian immigrants. In 1995, Vinoteca di Monica opened, located at 143 Richmond Street. This Italian eatery features a delicious variety of pasta, pizza, fish and meat dishes by Chef Jorge Mendoza-Iturralde. Expect your visit to Vinoteca di Monica to be a relaxed, European-style dinner where the diner is expected to linger over the meal, with no one rushing anyone to move along. Next door to this is Monica's Pasta Shop, a deli of delights that features Monica's famous homemade pasta. Additionally, sandwiches, pizzas and salads are available to go. Monica's tiny sister trattoria, aptly named Monica's Trattoria, is located nearby at 67 Prince Street. This Italian eatery is full of charm, with a brick interior and an old-country feel. The menu highlights Monica's *speciale* dishes, featuring homemade pasta from chefs Patrick and Frank Mendoza. Be sure to start with a caprese salad. Part of Monica's Mercato and Salumeria is Monica's Mercato Pizza, located off Noyes Place. Next to the market is the takeout pizza shop. Look for the painted sign pointing to the door. The subterranean pizza place is actually located beneath the Mercato. Grab the pie to go, as this tiny place has no room to eat inside.

For many, the ultimate Monica's experience is not at one of the sit-down establishments, though. The sandwiches at Monica's Mercato and Salumeria are legendary. The salumeria, or deli, originally was a place for the Mendoza family to sell their cured meats. The outcry from the public was so strong that they began putting their meats in sandwiches. The market expanded to the spotless storefront on 130 Salem Street in 2016. Even with this new location, expect lines out the door to try the famous Italian sandwiches. The classic Italian, with its layers of salami, prosciutto and mortadella, is among

Monica's Mercato is one of the many "Monica's" restaurants in the North End. *Jaclyn Lamothe.*

the bestsellers here. With the right amount of meat, cheese, vegetables and crusty bread, it is the perfect Italian. At Monica's, the meat is sliced in front of the customer and the bread is baked that morning.

The Monica restaurant group is owned and operated by brothers Jorge, Pat and Frank Mendoza. Although the family moved to the North End from Argentina in 1984, their mother, Monica, is from Northern Italy, hence the source of their love of Italian food. In homage to Mama, Monica was the name they chose. Monica's restaurants run the gamut from date-night special to a quick and easy sandwich or pizza. No matter what kind of Italian food you are looking for, Monica's fits the bill. Walking through the North End today, it is hard not to stumble into one of Monica's fine restaurants.

PASTRY

Although the North End is world renowned for its authentic Italian eateries, the one food item most closely associated with the neighborhood has to be the cannoli. The perfect cannoli's crispy shell is full of the best ricotta, some dipped in chocolate or accented with chocolate chips. The great debate in Boston has to do with which bakery makes the best. Granted, cannoli is such a popular dessert option that many North End restaurants make their own. Of course, many bakeries do too. For this contest though, we are sticking with the North End heavyweights in terms of name recognition. All of these certainly fit the category of "classic," as Mike's Pastry, the "youngest" bakery on the block, opened way back in 1946.

Mike's Pastry is certainly the most well known in the city. It would not be a night out in Boston without seeing scores of tourists (and locals) marching through downtown or on the T holding their Mike's Pastry boxes, signature white boxes with blue lettering, tied with a bow. Also vying for the "best cannoli" title is Modern Pastry, almost as well known and located just down the street. Expect long lines for a cannoli on weekend evenings. It has been around since 1930. The final is Bova's, the most off the beaten path (but still very close to the heart of the neighborhood). Bova's has been around since 1926 and is able to satisfy your sweet tooth twenty-four hours a day.

In chronological order, here's how the Big Three stack up.

Bova's Bakery, 1926

Bova's Bakery is certainly a contender for best cannoli and bakery in Boston. A. Bova and Sons Bakery is located at the corner of Salem and Prince Streets, at 74–76 Prince Street. Unlike Mike's and Modern, which are located on the main drag of Hanover Street, Bova's location is slightly off the tourist's beaten path. Not that it is far away, as this is only one block from Hanover Street.

Antonio Bova arrived in the United States in 1890, an immigrant from Reggio, the capital of the region of Calabria in Southern Italy. After honing his skills as a baker, including working at the Parziale's Bakery next to the present location of Bova's, Bova opened his own bakery in 1926. Originally located at 79 Prince Street, its address is now 134 Salem Street. The restaurant has stayed in the Bova family, as members of the fourth generation, Antonio's great-grandsons, help run it. Antonio Bova also ran the Calia, later the New England Bakery.

Some folks say that Bova's has the best cannoli in Boston. The dessert is smaller than the monstrous Mike's and comes in eight flavors. In addition to sweets such as biscotti, whoopie pie and tiramisu, Bova's also bakes bread and pizza. The interior shouts authentic Italian bakery, with large display cases of their creations and hot foods as well. There are also shelves lined with other goodies to choose from. The large Bova family still owns and operates the bakery, as they have since 1926.

Modern Pastry, 1930

Modern Pastry, another of the Big Three cannoli bakeries, is located at 257 Hanover Street. Another bakery with long lines on weekend nights, it also prides itself on the cannoli. These delicate treats are decidedly smaller than its friendly rival down the street, but some say they are tastier. In addition to the cannoli, the bakery is also known for its cakes, candy and other kinds of pastries. The owner of Modern Pastry was the late Giovanni "John" Picariello, who passed away at the age of eighty-seven in 2013. Modern also operates a second location in Medford, just north of Boston. It expanded the store in 2017, and the establishment is cash only.

Modern Pastry is one of the "Big Three" North End bakeries. *Jaclyn Lamothe.*

Modern Pastry's expansion left it almost unrecognizable to me. I can remember the way it was, a narrow space with one long line. The addition has made room for tables to eat at. Similar to Bova's, they sell other goodies too, including hot food such as pizza. There is also a secret bar, Modern Underground. Look for the sign pointing down the stairs to venture down there. It includes a full beverage menu, pub grub and televisions. It seems as if it is an old-fashioned speakeasy, as it would never be known that an establishment of this kind is located below street level underneath one of the city's most treasured old-school Italian bakeries.

Mike's Pastry, 1946

Mike's Pastry, noted for its storefront with large windows to see inside, is situated just down the street from Modern at 300 Hanover Street. Hands down, this bakery is the most famous not only in the North End but also in the city of Boston. As far as cannoli goes, many claim that Mike's is the best. In size, they are much larger than those of the other bakeries. The bakery was started by Michael Mercogliano. He was an Italian immigrant who arrived in the North End at twelve years old and started working at his cousin's bakery. Mercogliano passed away in 2012 at ninety years old. Mike's Pastry currently is owned by Angelo Papa, Mike's stepson.

Walking into Mike's when it's busy can be an overwhelming experience for the senses. First, the line is often out the door and down the sidewalk. Reaching the counter, it is hard to choose from the many styles of cannoli that range from the traditional to Oreo, pistachio or chocolate. The cannoli at Mike's are large, so make sure you leave room for one after a large plate of pasta. There are many other treats to choose from as well. Cookies, pizzelles, gelati, cheesecake—everything is so tempting! When it is busy, the bakery staff are running around filling orders and taking items out of the display case, which can add to the hectic pace. Mike's cannoli are filled daily, and the shells are handmade. Mike's Pastry is a known favorite of many celebrities, one true fan being former president Bill Clinton.

The original North End location has been joined by three branches: Harvard Square, Assembly Square in Somerville and TD Garden in Boston. During my recent visit to the original Mike's in the North End, I discovered that there are now five different lines leading to the counter, leaving no space in the bakery to peruse or dawdle.

And the Winner Is…

I have taken the cannoli challenge, sampling cannoli from each of these Boston stalwarts. To be fair, I opted for the plain cannoli with ricotta filling. Mike's certainly has the largest cannoli. If you are someone who likes quantity, go for Mike's. Modern was a similar consistency to Mike's; both were quite sweet. Modern's shell was crunchier than Mike's. Bova's was less sweet than the other two. At first, this gave it the nod for my favorite. Although I really enjoyed the very crispy shell, the filling was almost lost in it, as the shell dominated the filling.

To make matters more confusing, I also purchased three ricotta-filled cannoli with chocolate chips for the second round. Here I could not tell, for they were all delectable. I did realize though that I prefer my cannoli with chocolate chips. Some folks swear by one over the others, but personally, I think they are all great. Bova traditionally has less of a line than the other two. Mike's has multiple lines and moves fast. Take your pick; you will not leave unhappy, and if you are like me, go try all three!

Boxes of cannoli. *Jaclyn Lamothe.*

Irish Pubs around the City

If there is one ethnicity that comes to mind when speaking of Boston, it has to be Irish. Portrayed in movies such as *The Departed* and *Good Will Hunting*, the Irish of Boston have been glorified on the silver screen and written about in books such as the autobiography *All Souls* by Michael Patrick MacDonald and almost every Dennis Lehane novel. The Irish of Boston have made their way into the consciousness of mainstream America. And heck, even the professional basketball team is the Celtics! Also, folks who have never set foot in Beantown have heard of "Southie."

Typically, the Southie references have a negative connotation of gangs, violence or even racial undertones in reference to the busing protests of the 1970s. The prototypical Boston brogue, as spoken by Ben Affleck and Matt Damon in *Good Will Hunting*, is alive and well. Today's Southie is a far cry from the gang-ridden streets of yore. It is now an upscale, trendy neighborhood full of high-priced condominiums, boutiques and gastropubs.

The Irish connection permeates the city, not just in South Boston. Dorchester has long been associated with the Irish as well. Even the biggest band to come out of Boston in the last few decades, the Dropkick Murphys, are originally from this 'hood. To boot, Boston's most famous twentieth-century son, President John F. Kennedy, was also of Irish descent.

As far as restaurants go, Irish pubs are not confined to only the predominantly Irish ethnic neighborhoods of South Boston and Dorchester. An Irish pub can be found in practically every section of town, from neighboring Brookline to the heart of downtown Boston. Past and present

Expect to see many Irish pubs in Boston, such as the Black Rose. *Jaclyn Lamothe.*

names such as the Blarney Stone, the Purple Shamrock and Kinsale are all monikers that reference the country of origin.

Along with pubs that feature stick-to-your-ribs meals such as beef stew, shepherd's pie and fish and chips, many of the following establishments are known for pouring "Irish," which means Guinness. Unlike most beers, which are simply dispensed via tap, pouring the perfect Guinness is an art form. The stout beer should be poured holding the glass at a forty-five-degree angle, following a settling process. After that, it gets topped off. A bartender in the know will only serve it this way. It is common to find the Irish pubs mentioned here staffed by immigrants from the Emerald Isle or from established Boston Irish families.

J.J. FOLEY'S CAFÉ, 1909

J.J. Foley's Café, located at 117 East Berkeley Street in the South End, is an Irish-owned pub that is so historic it is from a time when an immigrant-owned restaurant was frowned upon, not a celebration of culture that is so present in Irish pubs today. Dating from 1909, it predates Prohibition and was known to be a fine shoe store during the years from 1920 to 1933. It was opened by Jerry Foley, an Irish immigrant from County Kerry who arrived in America at fifteen years old. Today's restaurant is owned and operated by the third and fourth generations of Foleys. Jerry Foley and his sons—Michael, Jeremiah, Patrick and Brendan—are in charge today. The waitstaff and bartenders are known for their handsome attire, the classic white shirt and tie of yore.

J.J. Foley's Café has morphed from a neighborhood bar to a pub. It used to be a popular hangout for *Boston Herald* reporters and employees, whose headquarters was formerly in the South End, and Boston cops who also had their headquarters close by. It has also been an establishment favored by politicians, including past mayors Ray Flynn, the notorious James Michael Curley and current mayor Marty Walsh. Most of the orders in earlier decades were a beer and a shot. The South End at that time was considered seedy, much less desirable than it is today. Now, Foley's is known for its food, with appetizers, burgers, pizza and sandwiches lining the menu. Patrons of Foley's now opt for the pub grub with a craft beer or a well-designed cocktail. The restaurant is gorgeous, with its cozy deep wood interior. It has a restaurant side and a bar side, exuding a friendly atmosphere for everyone. To keep up with the changing South End, which in the twenty-first century is a trendy and expensive neighborhood, Foley's was updated by adding a kitchen in 2007. Foley's sign is iconic with its coat of arms, and the restaurant inside is lined with memorabilia of Boston Irish.

There is a second location of J.J. Foley's, J.J. Foley's Bar and Grill, on Kingston Street in downtown Boston. This has similar pub grub and is known for its Guinness but does not have the same aesthetic as the South End pub. It is owned by Jerry's cousin Jim. The signs on the two establishments are the same, although they are not one and the same restaurant. Instead of sister restaurants, they are more like cousins. Even though this location is not as old as the South End Foley's, it has still been around for more than fifty years—not too shabby!

THE PLOUGH AND STARS, 1969

Although the Plough and Stars is known as much as a music venue as it is an Irish pub, no one can argue with the quality of the food and the ability to find a fine pour of Guinness at this Cambridge institution. On the music side of things, this venue has seen the likes of Jeff Buckley and Spider John Koerner grace the stage. The bluesy, hip-hop, funky, folky G. Love and Special Sauce were the house band here in the 1990s before they invaded college radio airwaves and MTV. G. Love, originally from Philadelphia, still calls Massachusetts home today. Another group, Treat Her Right, had a residency earlier. Members of this band, including vocalist Mark Sandman, would go on to form the acclaimed underground alternative group Morphine.

The name "The Plough and Stars" is in reference to the play of the same name written by the playwright Sean O'Casey. Although patrons flock here for the food and the live music, the establishment has been a bit of a cultural and political hotspot over the last fifty-plus years. Among those who spent time there are musicians such as Rock and Roll Hall of Fame musician Van Morrison, who is rumored to have written at least some of his album *Astral Weeks*, the zenith moment of a storied career, here. John Hume, Nobel Peace Prize winner for helping negotiate a cease of the Troubles between Northern Ireland and Ireland; author Phillip Roth; blues musician Bonnie Raitt; and Lawrence Ferlinghetti, poet and owner of City Lights Books in San Francisco, have all graced this establishment.

Even more interesting than the musicians or patrons of the Plough and Stars is the story of the owners. Peter and Padraig O'Malley are notable in their own right and have been the owners nearly since the beginning. Padraig is a world-renowned peacemaker who has helped broker peace in his native Ireland and other troubled spots around the globe, including South Africa, Nigeria and Iraq. The Plough and Stars was even the location of early discussions between opposing paramilitary forces during the Troubles. Additionally, he is a professor and the author of many books. The documentary film *The Peacemaker* is about O'Malley. Brother Peter and writer DeWitt Henry established the influential literary magazine *Ploughshares* at the pub in 1971. This magazine has published such literary luminaries as Stephen King, David Foster Wallace and Tim O'Brien. Throughout its history, the Plough has been a meeting space for Cambridgian free thinkers and Harvard scholars, bohemians and blue-collar workers. The clientele runs the gamut, and while many other such pubs, restaurants and bars come and go and the makeup of Central Square changes, the Plough and Stars remains. Peter's son Gabriel now owns the pub.

As far as the menu goes, the food at Plough and Stars goes far beyond the average Irish pub. Actually, other than the Irish breakfast on the brunch menu, this establishment does not reflect traditionalism in any way. Tacos, Brussels sprouts, catfish, quesadillas and salads are indicative of this extensive menu. The current executive chef is Jim Seery, and the manager is Michael O'Leary. The small Plough and Stars remains a remarkable and viable pub more than fifty years after its founding. With its wood-lined interior and friendly atmosphere, it is a slice of Boston history. If only these walls could talk! The Plough and Stars is located at 912 Massachusetts Avenue in Cambridge.

THE BLACK ROSE, 1976

Once upon a time in the city of Boston, there was not an Irish pub on the corner of every street. Now ubiquitous, the Irish pub was a rare sight. What is said to be the first Irish pub is what many also call the best: the Black Rose, a traditional Irish pub located in the heart of the Financial District, very close to the tourist hub of Faneuil Hall.

The Black Rose's history dates back to 1976, when owners Phil Sweeney and Richard McHugh decided to open the pub. The Black Rose or, in Gaelic, *Roisin Dubh*, which translates to "small black rose," is known to pour the perfect pint of Guinness. The name is in reference to the fact that Ireland was dubbed a "black rose" under its occupation by England. The pub is open every day of the year and features live Irish music every night of the week. Along with that, other well-known Irish musicians have made appearances at the Black Rose, including James Galway, the Chieftains and even U2.

Don't worry; the menu at the Black Rose accompanies the perfect pint of Guinness or a Jameson Irish Whisky on the rocks very well. Expect Irish and regional classics—beef stew meets lobster. Fish and chips, Irish breakfasts and bangers and mash are other popular menu choices. The pub is located on the bottom floor, with the dining room on the second floor. The interior is beautifully designed with lovely woodwork. The exterior is accentuated with the traditional colors of Ireland, green and orange. It is an everyman's pub: City Hall and State Street employees mingle with tourists and college students. The Black Rose became an apprenticeship of sorts for Irish bartenders. Many bartenders learned how to pour the perfect Guinness at the Black Rose before venturing off and opening up their own establishments.

Many of the workers at the Black Rose come from Ireland originally. Today, the restaurant is part of the larger Glynn Hospitality Group. The pub was sold in 1984 to P.J. Glynn, who started the Glynn Hospitality Group.

Sweeney worked for the company until he retired as a manager and passed away in 2014. Paul Wilson, who is the operations manager for the Glynn Hospitality Group, is originally from Dublin, Ireland, and has worked for them for decades, first at the Purple Shamrock when he was younger. P.J. Glynn himself was an immigrant from the county of Galway to the United States in the mid-twentieth century. The Glynn Hospitality Group owns a number of popular Boston establishments, including Brownstone, Coogan's, Clery's, Dillon's, Sterling's, Central Wharf Company, Sports Grille Boston and Granary Tavern. In the past, highlights of their portfolio include the Purple Shamrock, Jose McIntyre's and Hurricane O'Reilly's. Many of their holdings are also Irish pubs.

FLANN O'BRIEN'S, 1989

Flann O'Brien's, colloquially known as simply Flann's, is a venerable, authentic Irish pub in the Mission Hill neighborhood of Boston. Flann O'Brien's is named after the pen name of Irish writer Brian Nolan. Located just off Brigham Circle, only a few blocks from the Fenway region of colleges—including Northeastern University, Massachusetts College of Art and Design and Wentworth Institute of Technology, among others— it draws a significant college crowd. Flann's, though, attracts folks from all walks of life due to its pub grub, numerous draft beer options (including Irish staples such as Guinness, Murphy's and Smithwick's) and other local libations from breweries, including Harpoon and Samuel Adams, along with its jovial atmosphere.

Literally a corner bar, Flann's straddles Tremont and Wigglesworth Streets. From the outside, the pub's façade includes impressive stonework, which is also present inside. The striking red door greets patrons who make sure to pay homage to the statue of a figure toasting with a pint of presumably Guinness above the doorway. Cozy with a dark interior, Flann's also has a fireplace to warm up a cold Boston winter day. The menu includes traditional options such as burgers, an Irish breakfast and fish and chips. On the nontraditional side, there is also a well-regarded appetizer of potstickers. Many patrons opt for the daily special. At under six dollars currently, the daily burger specialty rotates but always pleases and is quite the bargain. Flann's is also known for its Guinness Breakfast Challenge. This is so outrageous that it was actually featured on the Travel Channel program *Man Versus Food*, where host Casey Webb tries to devour the whole Irish breakfast. This meal is enormous, including such items as eggs, white and black pudding, Irish sausage, bacon, home fries, Irish baked beans—and that is just the tip of the iceberg for this meal. It is available during brunch hours on the weekend. Eat all that in under half an hour and get a free T-shirt; add a pint of Guinness, and they will throw in a Flann's hat.

Flann's was opened in 1989 by Irish immigrant Finbarr "Butch" Murray, who had experience in the bar business in Ireland. Co-owner and manager Tony O'Brien is also from Ireland. Like a coat of many colors, Flann's wears many hats. It's a cozy Irish pub where you can sip a Guinness while reading the paper, as well as a family-friendly pub with great food for all ages. It's a college hangout with a DJ leading the party-like atmosphere, a host of weekly trivia nights and a place to shoot pool. Basically, Flann's can fit your mood and service a diverse clientele depending on the day and time.

THE BANSHEE, 1990

This Dorchester pub is known for the broadcasting of a variety of games to its Irish sports–loving crowd. From futbol, or soccer to us Americans, and rugby to Gaelic football and hurling, the Banshee is the premier destination for European sports fans in Boston. For American sports fans, don't worry, the Banshee still airs the Sox, the Celts, the Bs and the Pats. The menu is more diverse than most Irish pubs. Of course, expect solid pub grub, including burgers, mac and cheese and sandwiches, but this Irish pub is famous for its tacos, egg rolls and Asian fried cauliflower. Guinness is available on draft, but the Banshee also has craft beer offerings and an extensive mixed drink menu for those not "drinking Irish." The Banshee is located at 934 Dorchester Avenue.

MR. DOOLEY'S, 1991

Heading to the Financial District, Mr. Dooley's is heralded for its perfect Guinness pour. More than that, this authentic Irish pub keeps patrons coming back time and time again. On St. Patrick's Day, the old country–style atmosphere churns out plates upon plates of corned beef and cabbage. Its location at 77 Broad Street in Boston puts Mr. Dooley's at the heart of downtown. Visitors typically use "Boston" in reference to Dooley's since there was another branch of the pub in the South Shore of Massachusetts.

Mr. Dooley's is a popular Irish pub. *Jaclyn Lamothe.*

Miles south in the coastal town of Cohasset was a branch of Mr. Dooley's that closed in 2021. The menu consists of Irish pub favorites, including fish and chips, bangers and mash and shepherd's pie. Given its proximity to Boston Harbor, Dooley's also has seafood options, as well as traditional pub fare such as burgers, salads and sandwiches.

The restaurant dates back to 1991, when it was established by John Joe Somers. His vision was for a slice of Ireland within the cityscape of Boston. As in many of the most traditional Irish pubs in the city, in addition to the "perfect pour" of Guinness, live Irish music is common here. Somers was nineteen when he emigrated from Ireland. Since the death of Somers, his family has taken over the establishment. Known as the Somers Pubs, the family has branched out into the ownership of more than a handful of Irish pubs in the Boston area. The collection of Irish pubs includes Mr. Dooley's, the historic Green Dragon Tavern (also included in this book), Durty Nelly's, Hennessey's, Upstairs at Hennessey's and Paddy O's.

THE DRUID, 1994

In Cambridge's Inman Square, the Irish pub to visit is the Druid. Entering the Druid, located at 1357 Cambridge Street, feels as if you have walked into a pub in Dublin. The dark wood–paneled interior is complemented well with a perfect Guinness pour, live entertainment and a menu with staples such as fish and chips, beef stew and shepherd's pie. This pub is known for its delicious menu options. For a real slice of Ireland, try the Druid. Its diminutive size is reminiscent of a wee hole-in-the-wall from the old country. Many patrons flock to the Druid for the authentic live Irish music. The Druid has won numerous accolades from area mainstay publications such as *Boston Magazine.*

EMMET'S PUB, 1995

How can a pub on Beacon Street in Boston be considered hidden? With its address, 6 Beacon Street, in the midst of downtown Boston, between the State House and Tremont Street, it is located close to many popular destinations but tucked away just enough to be slightly off the beaten path. Emmet's is a fine Irish pub whose menu includes Guinness beef stew, a collection of sandwiches, shepherd's pie and clam chowder. It is also known for the live traditional music that is often heard within its walls. The interior is lined with dark wood with light walls. This cozy Irish pub is worth taking the trip past the Massachusetts State House for a pint of Guinness and a hearty meal.

THE BURREN, 1996

For the classic Irish pub to visit while in Somerville, the Burren is it. The Burren takes its name from a rocky natural landscape in County Clare known for its oft-photographed dolmen, a megalithic tomb that dates from a few thousand years BCE and is used as the logo for the namesake pub. Among the popular dishes here are the shepherd's pie, bangers and mash and fish and chips. The beef stew's broth is made with Guinness.

The Burren is also known as a live music venue. Live music in various forms includes but is not limited to folk, jazz and bluegrass, as well as traditional Irish music. The Back Room at the Burren even has its own album of collected live tracks from this venue, including selections from Irish musicians Sharon Shannon and Andy Irvine. Traditional music is the soul of the Burren, as husband-and-wife owners Louise Costello and Tommy McCarthy are accomplished musicians in their own right. Costello is an accordionist and banjo player, and McCarthy is a fiddler.

The Burren is located at 247 Elm Street in the heart of Somerville's Davis Square. Although Davis Square is a hip neighborhood in the uber-cool Somerville, the Burren's tenure began before the neighborhood became the revitalized square that it is presently. The walls are lined with pictures and painted a warm red. The Burren is larger than such area Irish pubs as the Plough and Stars and the Druid but retains its coziness.

Chinatown

Of all of Boston's ethnic neighborhoods, among the most authentic is Chinatown. A true enclave that was once tucked away in the shadow of two major highways is now threatened by the ever-growing development, commercially and residentially, of downtown Boston. Chinatown is coping with change as a neighborhood, with its strong roots in the past adapting to the modern world of the present without losing its identity, to keep Chinatown an enclave of traditionalism while being able to stay relevant. Chinatown is trying to avoid ultimate gentrification, which would leave the Asian imprint in this community as something of the past. The neighborhood is looking to keep its cultural roots within a twenty-first-century Boston.

The official entrance to Chinatown is through the gate on Beach Street, one of the neighborhood's major streets. The gate was a present from Taiwan in 1982. Along with the lion statuary located in the same plaza, this is the symbol of Boston's Chinatown. Through the gate is a bustling neighborhood where many of the restaurants' and shops' signage are written in Chinese, and English is not the first language spoken. For a small neighborhood, Chinatown packs a lot in. Its population is roughly four thousand persons. In the twenty-first century, the name "Chinatown" is a bit of a misnomer, as the population also includes individuals from other Asian countries. It is bordered by the Theater District, the South End and Downtown Crossing. Not long ago, Chinatown included the notorious Combat Zone, Boston's red-light district, its home for adult entertainment and all that accompanies it. When the seedy Scollay Square was bulldozed to make way for the

The Chinatown Gate greets visitors to the neighborhood. *Author's photo.*

Government Center plaza, the unsavory entertainment moved south to this neighborhood. Only traces of the Combat Zone remain, with two adult performance venues still in operation in this region. The heart of the Combat Zone was on Washington Street, delineated as the area between Essex and Kneeland Streets.

Major streets, including Essex, Beach and Kneeland, cross through Chinatown, but the heart of it lies within the smaller roads such as Tyler and Hudson Streets, which are lined with restaurants and shops. Classic Chinese eateries, including the oldest in the neighborhood, China Pearl, along with other venerable favorites Peach Farm and Winsor Dim Sum Café, are all located on Tyler Street. These streets are not only rooted in the past, but newer restaurants such as the ever-popular Shojo are also located on Tyler Street.

With the Orange Line providing public transit to and from Chinatown, a visit here showcases not only authentic restaurants but also markets and stores. The neighborhood began in 1875 in a region that was once known as South Cove. Prior to this, in colonial Boston, this region was where the Liberty Tree was planted. Liberty Plaza commemorates the planting, located at the corner of Washington and Boylston Streets. Other groups to inhabit this neighborhood of South Cove include the Irish, Jewish and Syrian, as well as other Arab ethnicities.

The original Chinese immigrants were brought in to work in the mills of Lawrence, Massachusetts, north of Boston. Workers in this factory city were on strike, with the Chinese immigrants acting as strikebreakers. After uprooting themselves to work in the factories, once the strike was over, the Chinese immigrants were promptly laid off. The immigrants migrated once again, this time to the city of Boston. In the South Cove area, a shantytown of sorts known as Ping On Alley was set up. In 1989, Oliver Place's name was officially changed to Ping On Alley. There is a historic marker detailing this at the corner of Ping On Alley and Essex Street on the side of a building. Chinese immigration was further stalled due to the Chinese Exclusion Act of 1882. Eventually, with the act's repeal in 1943, post–World War II Boston witnessed an uptick in Chinese immigration. Beginning in the 1960s, individuals of other Asian ethnicities also settled in this area.

Although Chinatown was once delineated by the Mass Pike underpass and the monstrous Southeastern Expressway, Route 93's elevated highway, it is now seamlessly woven into the fabric of the larger city on the whole due to the demolition of the overhead expressway (which is now subterranean due to the Big Dig construction project). What has not changed is what to expect in Chinatown, and as far as this book goes, that is great food. Try a mooncake at Hing Shing Pastry at 67 Beach Street or a fruit cake at Eldo Cake House at 36 Harrison Avenue. Another Chinatown must-try is a dim sum experience. At some restaurants, the small dishes are wheeled around tableside by servers pushing a cart. This is the experience at China Pearl, which will be explained further below. Try a sampling of the best in Chinese food with dumplings, steamed buns and rolls as dim sum. Dim sum is a series of small dishes and is a Cantonese specialty, traditionally eaten for lunch or breakfast. Another Chinatown classic eatery is Peach Farm at 4 Tyler Street. The tables at this Cantonese restaurant come with a lazy Susan so every member of the party can try the delicious offerings. Peach Farm is known for its seafood dishes, including the exotic, such as snails and surf clam. For a neighborhood rooted in the cuisine of Asian cultures, there is a diverse selection of choices. From Cantonese to Chinese barbecue, Vietnamese to Korean, the choices are endless. One of the funkier places, reflecting modern Asian cuisine, is Double Chin, which is known for its cube toast, outrageous hollowed-out brioche served French

Chinatown is known for its large and vibrant signage. *Jaclyn Lamothe.*

toast style, a basis for an ice cream sundae of sorts with toppings including cereal, ice cream and Pocky (thin chocolate-covered biscuits). Double Chin is located at 86 Harrison Avenue. Clearly, when visiting Chinatown, you will not leave hungry!

CHINA PEARL, 1960S

In addition to crowded streets, Chinese characters and a world of food, Chinatown is also known for its retro signs that greet many of the neighborhood's restaurants. One of the largest and most famous is the one-story-tall sign of China Pearl, with its distinct black lettering on a yellow background, jutting out from the building at 9 Tyler Street. Trying the dim sum is a must at China Pearl. There are countless items to choose from, but some of the most popular include pork and shrimp shumai, barbecue pork bun and sticky rice in lotus leaf. Other menu items include rice noodles, congee (a Chinese rice porridge) and an array of desserts. Some of the more adventurous selections include shark fin dumplings (which are not actually made with shark fin), candied lotus root, chicken feet, tripe (cow stomach) and salt and pepper squid. This is truly an authentic experience. More recognizable dishes such as General Tso's chicken, fried rice and lo mein are also options.

The restaurant began in the 1960s and is the oldest restaurant in operation in Chinatown. It was started by Frank and Billy Chin. Ricky Moy purchased China Pearl in the late 1980s. He had worked at China Pearl at age fourteen as a busboy. He owned a few local businesses, including a barbecue bakery and Ho Yuen Ting, later known as the Best Little Restaurant. For the Moys, China Pearl is a family affair, with many family members presently or historically employed there. Brian Moy, Ricky's son, has been involved in the restaurant business since he was a mere child and has taken over the mantle of restaurateur premier in this neighborhood.

Under the tutelage of Ricky Moy, China Pearl started serving dim sum, which it is still known for today. The interior of the restaurant is bathed in red. It is a large, bright space, in which guests feel welcome. Dim sum carts glide their way around the restaurant. There is also a salad bar and takeout options. China Pearl has employed many recent immigrants and teaches the staff English. China Pearl is also known for its late hours, closing at 3:30 a.m.

China Pearl has a second location at 237 Quincy Avenue in Quincy, Massachusetts, just a few miles south of Boston; it opened in the mid-2000s. This community is known for its large Asian population, including many Chinese families relocated from Chinatown.

BRIAN MOY'S SHOJO, 2012

Shojo was opened in 2012 by Brian Moy, whose family owns China Pearl. Moy had worked at China Pearl since he was ten years old. Moy's Shojo (9A Tyler Street) is just next door to China Pearl, and whereas China Pearl features dim sum and a wide variety of traditional Chinese food, Shojo is a hip, albeit nontraditional, Asian restaurant. Moy also opened BLR by Shojo in 2016, which offers new spins on the traditional food of Chinatown. The original Best Little Restaurant was opened in 1982 and run by his family. He also operates Ruckus, another restaurant, next to these. Moy represents the face of the new Chinatown, someone who is proud of his heritage and the neighborhood, who is looking to preserve the culture in the face of gentrification with the construction of nearby sparkling high-rises and Tufts Medical Center. He puts a modern spin on his food with a welcoming, hip vibe at his restaurants, but at the same time, he brings in elements of the past.

Little Armenia: East Watertown

Boston is synonymous with its ethnic neighborhoods, such as the North End and Chinatown. One ethnic group with a large presence in Boston but less in the culinary limelight is Armenians. The Boston area has a relatively large concentration of Armenian Americans, some whose roots trace back to the late nineteenth and early twentieth centuries and others who are more recent arrivals.

The nickname for East Watertown is "Little Armenia," and it consists of a collection of Armenian cultural institutions, including restaurants, stores, bakeries, churches and schools. Also in Watertown is the Armenian Cultural and Educational Center, which is the largest Armenian museum outside Armenia itself. Unlike other chapters that solely focus on the food but intersperse only a bit of historical background, this chapter dedicates a bit more space to understand the group of Armenians who live and work in Watertown, the reason for their migration and their influence within the community.

To clarify, Watertown is a separate city from Boston, not a neighborhood, although it is located geographically close. Watertown is bordered by Cambridge on the east and across the Charles River from Newton and the Brighton neighborhood of Boston on the south. Belmont is north of it, and Waltham is to the west. Today's Watertown is densely populated and known for the old Watertown Arsenal, which was since developed into the Arsenal Mall and is now called the Arsenal Yards, a mixed-use residential and commercial center in this location. It is also known for the Watertown Mall located across the street. Watertown is urban in nature, with a similar feel to neighboring Cambridge, Brighton, Belmont and Waltham, with a mix of residential neighborhoods and busy commercial thoroughfares.

Armenia is a country in eastern Asia that has undergone much strife and turmoil over the last 150 years. It borders Turkey on the west. The other countries that surround it include Georgia, Azerbaijan and Iran. Throughout its modern history, Armenians have been persecuted, including during the horrific Armenian Genocide, which took place during the years from 1915 to 1922 at the hands of the Ottoman Turks. In a volatile area of the world, Armenia's predominant religion is Christianity, which is different from many of its neighbors. During this genocide, an estimated 1.5 million Armenians were killed. During much of the twentieth century, Armenia was a satellite country of the Soviet Union. Truly, Armenians have faced much persecution at the hands of others throughout the country's recent history. Although Armenia is its own country, many Armenians live or have lived throughout the region, including a large populace in Turkey.

Armenians were living in the Ottoman Empire in present-day Turkey but were historically victims of prejudice due to their religion. They were thought of as inferior and had to pay a special non-Muslim tax. The expulsion, removal and deportation of Armenians within the borders of the Ottoman Empire was not the first time the government had tried to eradicate Armenians from within its borders. During the Armenian Massacre of 1894–96, the Turkish military, as well as civilians, exterminated their own Armenian countrymen since the Armenian population was looking for more rights within the empire.

The Young Turks, a revolutionary group, overthrew the sultan and his government and took power in Turkey in 1908. Once the initial hope that this group would be more sympathetic toward the plight of the Armenians was dashed, the Young Turks' true doctrine was soon realized. They were wary of anyone who was not Turkish, especially Christians. During World War I, the Ottoman Empire joined Germany and Austria-Hungary's Central Powers. The religious leaders of the Ottoman issued a holy war on Christians who were not on their side. Coupled with the fact that some Armenians joined the Russian army that sided with the Allies in World War I, the Ottoman government declared that the Armenians were traitors and needed to be eradicated. This led to the mass genocide of what some scholars believe to be around 1.5 million individuals. They were led on deportation marches out of their homeland, starved and shot. They faced all kinds of horrible extermination methods. To this day, the Turkish government has not recognized this genocide.

Unlike some other American immigrant groups, such as the Irish escaping the potato famine or others simply looking for a better life, the Armenian immigrants came here, in many cases, fleeing persecution. This is important background information regarding an ethnic neighborhood enclave such as that of East Watertown. The Armenian diaspora (a group of people who have moved to various parts of the world out of their original homeland) has taken people of Armenian descent all over the world. A large population is in California, but Watertown, Massachusetts, is noted for its community with strong ethnic ties, traditional foods, Armenian language spoken and Orthodox churches to serve its populace. Now let us take a look at the businesses and cuisine that make up "Little Armenia."

Along with the cultural center, churches and other public buildings, the heart of Watertown's Armenian community is alive in the markets, bakeries and grocery stores of the neighborhood. So much influence does this have that Armenians from all over New England travel to Watertown to shop for traditional ingredients that are used in Armenian recipes. Additionally, Watertown is home to many other Middle Eastern ethnicities, including Lebanese and Persian. Many Lebanese and Persian dishes are similar to Armenian, and some restaurants even feature Armenian dishes on their menus even though their primary cuisine is Persian.

The first Armenian immigrants migrated to the South End, as well as to Cambridgeport and Watertown, for work in factory jobs. Although they were facing persecution, the immigration continued until the United States limited Armenian immigration through the Immigration Act of 1924. The Hood Rubber Plant and the GE Plant were important employers for the Armenian immigrants in Watertown. Another employer was the Eastern Clothing Company, which still exists today, although it is solely a store and not a manufacturer.

The area known as Little Armenia is centered on Mount Auburn Street, a thoroughfare that connects Cambridge to Watertown. Noticing the names on the businesses in this area, clearly, it is not just "Smith" and "Jones" on the storefronts. The food—no matter if Armenian or other Middle Eastern—includes many spices and other popular items including grape leaves, pita bread and hummus. One item that is similar to an Armenian flatbread pizza is lamejun. This is available at many of the Watertown bakeries, cafés and stores.

One popular item at many area restaurants and bakeries is boreg, a cheese-stuffed pie made with phyllo dough. At some places, boreg will be spelled differently, with variations including "boereg" or "borag." No matter what, expect a cheesy phyllo dough that is a treat. Another famous dish is karniyarik, an eggplant stuffed and loaded with spices, tomatoes and meat, among other ingredients. Soorj is a highly potent Armenian coffee that is served in small cups and is available at Watertown-area establishments. Shish kebabs are also popular in Armenian restaurants, as are spinach pies. For dessert, you must try Armenian shortbread cookies and pahklava.

The following is a sampling of some of the most popular and authentic Armenian and Middle Eastern restaurants and stores in the Watertown area.

MASSIS BAKERY, 1938

One of the oldest still-running Watertown Armenian establishments is Massis Bakery. Massis is long known for its Armenian delights. Originally, this bakery was known as Aintab Lahmejune. Here, you can try dishes including the grape leaves, salads and lamejunes. (Lamejune is another word that has many spellings.) Pickled vegetables are also popular to buy here. Mamoul is a date- or nut-filled cookie that Massis Bakery is known for. Pahklava is a similar dessert to the Greek baklava, a layered phyllo dough pastry in which honey is used as a sweetener. Similar to pahklava is kataifi, which is made with phyllo dough that has been shredded instead of kept in sheets. A Farina cake is another popular dessert found here. Clearly, Massis Bakery is a popular stop for Armenian and Middle Eastern sweets. It offers fresh bakery items and prepared foods as well. It is also a great place to pick up an assortment of olives and cheeses. Falafel, kebabs and shawarma are spectacular sandwiches and are a must-try. Falafel is almost like a Middle Eastern gateway food. Full of flavor, these fried chickpea and spiced balls are served inside rolled pita bread with tomato, turnip pickles and romaine lettuce, all mixed with tahini sauce. For those who have never had Middle Eastern food of any kind, falafel is a great place to start. Similar to Sevan Bakery, Massis has food to go, a salad bar–style area and many other grocery items in this international market. Massis Bakery is located at 569 Mount Auburn Street in Watertown.

EASTERN LAMEJUN BAKERS, 1942

Another Armenian mainstay market and bakery is right over the Watertown border in Belmont. Even though it is technically in a different town, the bakery is literally located on the Watertown city line. The bakery was established by the Koundakjian family in 1942, and forty-two years later, the Dervartanian family took over and still owns it. Similar to other area Armenian bakeries and markets, Eastern Lamejun is a mix of groceries and delicious homemade prepared food to go, as well as delectable sweets. It also includes a salad bar–style counter with an outstanding array of olives. Of course, with "lamejun" in the name, the Armenian flatbread pizzas are outstanding. Eastern Lamejun Bakers is located at 145 Belmont Street.

SEVAN BAKERY, 1971

The Sevan Bakery, which is named for a river in Armenia, is a store, bakery and takeout establishment. The Armenian Chavushian family immigrated to Boston from Istanbul, Turkey, in 1979, but the store specializes in more than just Armenian food and is more of an international (especially Middle Eastern) market. Sevan Bakery was purchased by Margaret and Gabriel Chavushian in 1984. Although the family had no experience prior to opening a restaurant, they were food lovers who enjoyed cooking. Since their ownership began over thirty-six years ago, their proprietorship has been a success. Today, the bakery is co-owned by son Nuran. What a selection this store has! From meat pies and wraps to salads and sweets, there is clearly something for everyone here. Many Armenian restaurants have "mezes" on the menu, which are appetizers. At Sevan, these include dishes such as hummus, tabbouleh and baked eggplant. Expect many delicious flavors and spices at Sevan. Their menu is extensive, and the customer can order takeout as well as select ingredients to make their own dishes. Sevan has an extensive salad bar and deli counter, which will make it hard to choose what to take home. They also have a wine selection from around the world but feature many from the Middle East. Sevan Bakery is located at 599 Mount Auburn Street in Watertown.

ARAX MARKET, 1974

Another long-standing market in East Watertown's Coolidge Square is Arax Market. Similar to many such markets, Arax is family-owned. Elizabeth Bassmajian, her husband Hagop and her three brothers established Arax in 1974. Today, it is still in the family, with the Bassmajians' sons at the helm.

Even though the Bassmajians are Lebanese, many of the same flavors can be found at this market as at the Armenian bakeries such as Massis and Sevan. Arax combines produce and necessities with international foods, especially from the Middle East. It is known region-wide for its baked treats and also features an impressive cheese selection and hard-to-find produce. Visit Arax Market at 585 Mount Auburn Street in Watertown.

THESE MARKETS COMBINE ALL THE best of an eatery under one roof, with groceries with special focus on hard-to-find Middle Eastern ingredients, a serve-yourself salad bar, a bakery and homemade prepared foods such as sandwiches, salads and flatbreads. There are additionally many restaurants that are producing some amazing home-cooked Armenian and Middle Eastern cuisine. For a quick bite, try Fordee's Falafel at 555 Mount Auburn Street in Watertown; it's obvious from the name, it is known for its falafel. Other favorite restaurants that specialize in similar Middle Eastern cuisine in this area of Watertown include Jana Grill at 2 Watertown Street and Roksana's Persian Food at 133 Mount Auburn Street. Expect menu items such as hummus, tabbouleh, shish kebabs and more.

KAREEM'S, 1993/2012

One Syrian restaurant that has earned many accolades for a fine sit-down meal is Kareem's. Kareem's is located at 99 Common Street in Watertown. Chef Ahmad Yasin originally opened Kareem's at 600 Mount Auburn Street in the heart of East Watertown's Coolidge Square in 1993. The restaurant earned rave reviews and was open for about twenty years. Accolades included "best of" awards from *Boston Magazine* and high praise from *Zagat* and the *Boston Globe*. The original Kareem's was known for its grape leaves, fattoush and many vegetarian options when vegetarian dishes were not easily found on menus. Chef Yasin shuttered Kareem's in 2000 to spend his time cooking in a different realm. Instead of helming a restaurant, he worked catering and teaching the cooking of Syrian and Middle Eastern food. Much to the joy of area diners, Kareem's opened in a new location in 2012.

While many of the restaurants mentioned earlier are more in the vein of takeout spots, bakeries and markets, Kareem's is a fine dining restaurant. Chef Yasin focuses on flavor and healthful menu items. He still has many vegetarian options on the menu. For instance, kibbeh, which is a popular Middle Eastern meat dish, is available three ways: with lamb, with salmon or vegetarian. Just like in his original Kareem's, the fattoush salad is a hit. Fattoush is made with toasted pita or khubz with an array of greens, cucumbers, mint and tomatoes accompanied by a light lemony dressing. Popular appetizers include the hummus and baba ghanouj. Tabbouleh and the fattoush salad are crowd-pleasers. Although many of the entrées feature meats, including lamb, chicken or seafood, Kareem's vegetarian options are always available. And definitely try the orange blossom baklava for dessert.

EAST WATERTOWN'S COOLIDGE SQUARE, AROUND which many of these establishments are congregated, is only a stone's throw away from Watertown's most renowned place: Mount Auburn Cemetery. On a nice day, grab a lunch of sandwiches, salads and mezes from these fine Watertown restaurants, bakeries and groceries and have a picnic at the country's premier garden cemetery. Mount Auburn has winding roads through its scattered gravestones, along with lagoons and an observation tower, which makes it feel more like a museum or park than a cemetery.

Boston's Historic Taverns

The history of eighteenth-century Boston, known as the Cradle of the Revolution, is that of the events leading up to the American Revolution. With the likes of Boston luminaries such as Paul Revere, Samuel Adams and Joseph Warren instrumental in the nation's plea for independence, sites dedicated to their lives are essential aspects of Boston's history. Many of the historic locations of colonial Boston and sites connected to the Revolutionary War are found along the Freedom Trail, a two-and-a-half-mile trail that winds its way from Boston Common downtown to the Bunker Hill Monument in Charlestown. It passes by many important historic locales, such as the Paul Revere House, the Old South Meetinghouse and the Old State House.

Along the historic route, or in close proximity to it, are places where the likes of Revere, Adams and Warren held court. Not only were taverns neighborhood drinking establishments where the Founding Fathers were known to raise a pint or two, but many also were meeting spots, clandestine or not, for revolutionary activity.

Two of the most historic that are still standing and in use are Warren Tavern in Charlestown and the Bell in Hand on Union Street in Boston. Other famous taverns, including the Green Dragon, Salutation Tavern and Bunch-of-Grapes Tavern, are faded memories of Boston's past that long ago fell victim to demolition.

But doesn't the Green Dragon Tavern still exist today? Yes, kind of. Today's Green Dragon Tavern is located at 11 Marshall Street, on the same block that houses Union Oyster House and across from the Bell in Hand. Although the tavern plays on its history, the original was located close by on Union Street. The modern Green Dragon was founded in 1993.

GREEN DRAGON TAVERN, 1654/1993

The Green Dragon Tavern, which was built in 1654 and lasted until 1832, was the secret meeting place for the Sons of Liberty, which included Paul Revere, Samuel Adams and Joseph Warren. To posterity, it is known as the "Headquarters of the Revolution." The tavern became a Freemason Lodge in the mid-1760s and held the clandestine meetings of this group. Today's Green Dragon Tavern on Marshall Street, established in 1993, is known for pub grub, cold beer and live music. On the spot of the former tavern's location is a plaque commemorating it.

Left: The Freedom Trail connects historic sites (and classic restaurants) in Boston. *Jaclyn Lamothe*.

Right: The original Green Dragon Tavern was a meeting place for the Sons of Liberty. *Jaclyn Lamothe*.

WARREN TAVERN, 1780

Located at 2 Pleasant Street in Charlestown, Warren Tavern is one of the city's oldest establishments. It is named for Dr. Joseph Warren, a Harvard graduate and a member of the Sons of Liberty, who helped establish the Committee of Correspondence and was a Freemason. He was also known as the person who sent Paul Revere and William Dawes on the famous Midnight Ride. Dr. Warren was appointed major general and fought at the Battle of Bunker Hill, which ultimately led to his death on June 17, 1775. There is a statue of Warren near the Bunker Hill Monument inside the columned lodge located on the grounds. The lodge and monument are actually on Breed's Hill.

As far as Warren Tavern itself, it was erected in 1780, named after Dr. Joseph Warren, and is proclaimed as the oldest tavern in the state. It was known as Paul Revere's watering hole of choice, with George Washington its most famous patron. Charlestown was set ablaze by the British during the Revolutionary War. Upon its reconstruction, the tavern was one of the first

The historic Warren Tavern in Charlestown. *Ann Marie Lyons.*

buildings built. It was constructed in the Federal style by Captain Eliphelet Newell. George Washington and Paul Revere were also Freemasons. King Solomon's Masonic Lodge used the tavern as its meeting space.

The building's original run as a tavern ceased in 1813. After various uses, the wrecking ball loomed in the 1970s. Fortunately, in 1972, Alan and Ann Cunha and Neil and Ed Grennan reopened the tavern after rehabilitating the building.

Today, customers enjoy patronizing Warren Tavern for many more reasons than its history alone. Sure, eating a bowl of chowder and sipping a beer in the same spot as Revere and Washington is exciting, but Warren Tavern packs in the crowds due to its food and comfortable setting. The current general manager is John Harnett. Locals and tourists come to Warren Tavern. It has a dual identity as a neighborhood eatery and a tourist destination due to its historic relevance. Popular menu items include fish and chips, fish tacos, steak tips, burgers, lobster rolls and clam chowder. The interior includes a bar and dining room with wood floors and beams. It is a great spot to catch a Red Sox game on TV, listen to live music and enjoy a great meal. Make sure to try the acclaimed garlic mustard!

BELL IN HAND TAVERN, 1795

Back in downtown Boston, at 45 Union Street, where downtown meets the North End, is a collection of historic restaurants and bars, including Union Oyster House, the Green Dragon and the Bell in Hand Tavern. Dating from 1795, this tavern is actually where Benjamin Franklin's boyhood home was and is considered one of the oldest pubs in the country.

The name Bell in Hand is in reference to the occupation of original proprietor James "Jimmy" Wilson. He was the town crier. The job of a town crier was to announce the news of the day to the community. Wilson announced such major events in American history as the signing of the Declaration of Independence. The original location was in Pi Alley, where the old City Hall is today. Pi Alley still exists, bridging Court Street and Washington Street in downtown Boston close to the location of the Old State House. Pi Alley's cut-through connected the old City Hall to Newspaper Row, an area on Washington Street that was home to many of the city's newspapers. In 1844, the Bell in Hand moved to its current location on Union Street but retained the circa 1795 bar inside.

Due to Wilson's personal taste, no hard liquor was served at the Bell in Hand; only beer was allowed. The tavern was also known for a "two-mug beer": one mug for the liquid and one for the foam. The Bell in Hand today is known for fine pub grub, including wings, nachos, clam chowder and lobster rolls. Burgers with historic references include the "Freedom Trail Burger" and the "Sam Adams Burger." Try the Boston cream pie for dessert. Throughout its history, up through today, the Bell in Hand has always been a lively, communal gathering spot in Boston.

Boston Hipster Classics

As in any great city, Boston has its share of bohemian enclaves. Granted, with the ever-increasing real estate price tag, many of the artists who once inhabited neighborhoods such as Harvard Square in Cambridge, the South End and Davis Square in Somerville have been driven out in favor of young professionals, urban families and, to be blunt, those who can afford these desirable zip codes. Take Harvard Square, for instance. The 1960s Boston folk scene centered on Club 47. Club 47, a tiny basement music venue at 47 Palmer Street in Harvard Square, is now called Club Passim. In the 1960s, up-and-coming musicians, including Joan Baez, Joni Mitchell and Tom Rush, played here. With its university, bookstores, record stores and coffee shops, Harvard Square was the focal point of urban bohemians in the 1960s.

Through the latter half of the twentieth century, Boston as a city sprouted some of the most influential underground musicians. Rockers Aerosmith and Boston became household names, but many other influential groups also came out of Beantown. The Modern Lovers—fronted by the charismatic Jonathan Richman, who would go on to a storied career as a singer-songwriter in his own right—came from Boston. They even sang about their roots in tracks such as "Roadrunner," which namechecks Route 128; "Government Center"; and "Girl Friend," which mentions the Boston Museum of Fine Arts. Other members of the Modern Lovers would join successful New England bands the Cars and the Talking Heads. In the

1990s, the city was home to a successful indie rock scene, including bands such as the Lemonheads, Letters to Cleo and the Mighty Mighty Bosstones.

Even if the hipster quota of Boston has been driven into far-reaching neighborhoods in East Boston or Dorchester, the city still has an underground artistic presence that will never go away. From underground electronic music on such record labels as Moon Villain to open artist studios in Somerville and the South End, the arts scene is still thriving.

As far as restaurants go, there are presently and historically restaurants that are frequented by the artistic set. A few of these have become so ingrained in the community that they are established as classic restaurants. Among these are Charlie's Kitchen in Harvard Square and Bukowski's Tavern in the Back Bay. Don't worry; even if you want to visit the Boston area's finest hipster establishments, you need not wear your skinny jeans. At Charlie's Kitchen and Bukowksi's, everyone feels welcome and you will be able to indulge in tasty comfort food washed down with a frosty beer.

CHARLIE'S KITCHEN, 1951

From the interior's vinyl booths and long counter to the façade, which resembles a carnival booth with red and black block letters, you know you are in for an experience at Charlie's. The restaurant has multiple sections, including a diner restaurant downstairs, a lounge upstairs, a patio and a beer garden outside. Charlie's is best known for its unforgettable double cheeseburger. Of course, there are many variations of this, such as the Double Guinness cheeseburger and the Double Guacamole. Other popular menu items include grilled cheese and lobster. Charlie's Kitchen has this undeniable quality that makes it a hit with everyone. Even though it has a hip vibe, at the same time, it is completely retro and family-friendly. It literally wears all hats and is perfect for everyone, although maybe not for someone looking for fine dining. If that is what you are looking for though, just out the back door of Charlie's is the other restaurant that owner Paul Overgaag runs, the Red House, which features upscale entrées and interesting appetizers, with an emphasis on fresh fish. Both restaurants include farm-to-table ingredients from Charlie's Redhouse Farm, which he bought in 2009 in Winchendon, Massachusetts, over an hour's drive northwest of Cambridge near the New Hampshire border. With fresh produce, eggs and meat directly sourced from his farm, Charlie's also includes eco-friendly solar panels on the roof and uses compostable plastics. Even with an old-school feel, this Cambridge mainstay is progressive.

Charlie's Kitchen may be a hipster classic but is a comfortable eatery for everyone. *Author's photo.*

Charlie's Kitchen dates back to 1951. The original owner was Charlie Lambrose. Waitress Helen T. Metros was a waitress here for almost fifty years. Charlie's has served everyone from presidents to musicians, college students to retirees. The restaurant has won many accolades, including the best Harvard Square bar, the best dive bar and the best jukebox.

Charlie's Kitchen is located at 10 Eliot Street in Cambridge.

BUKOWSKI'S TAVERN, 1989

Poet and classic curmudgeon Charles Bukowski would be proud of this establishment bearing his name. The tavern puts an emphasis on beer and comfort food, with a brusque waitstaff. Although the address is in the Back Bay, the Ritz it ain't. It has the unique location of abutting a mega-story parking garage on one side and on the other side offering a picturesque view of the Mass Pike's steady stream of traffic below. With all of the architectural beauty that the Back Bay offers, Bukowski's has somehow found the one

Only Bukowski's could be located in the same structure as a parking garage. *Author's photo.*

spot that exudes drabness and functionality. From the street, this unassuming little red building provides a great contrast with the concrete surroundings.

The interior includes depictions and silhouettes of Old Buk. One would expect to see his ghost perched on a barstool, imbibing a cheap beer, or maybe that of Henry Chinaski, the character Mickey Rourke played in *Barfly*, the film somewhat based on Bukowski's life.

For its rough-and-tumble ways, Bukowski's is a classic restaurant. It has superior pub grub and an atmosphere that would make anyone feel comfortable. Hot dogs, burgers, fries and other classic comfort food are on the menu, along with a well-stocked beer selection. Despite its Charles Bukowski–esque reputation, even my parents felt more than comfortable as we dined here before a concert at the nearby Berklee Performance Center.

Its sister location, another Bukowski's, in Inman Square, opened in 2003 and shuttered in 2020, another victim of the COVID pandemic. In 2014, the sister restaurant came under the ownership of Boston restaurateur Brian Poe. Poe's other establishments include the Tip Tap Room, Poe's Kitchen at the Rattlesnake and Parish Café.

Bukowski's is located at 50 Dalton Street. If you're a local, try joining the mug club.

RIP: PEOPLE'S REPUBLIK

As one of many casualties of the COVID-19 pandemic, a prime hipster Cambridge establishment shuttered in 2021. If you are driving along Mass Ave in Cambridge's Central Square and notice one building that looks not like the others, you've stumbled onto People's Republik. Looking literally imposing from the outside, the uninformed would not have guessed that this was actually a bar and restaurant serving inventive pub grub. People's Republik's façade is draped in black with its name in red Soviet-style block letters. The interior featured images of Lenin, Che Guevara and Fidel Castro. The name was a play on the "People's Republic of Cambridge," a tongue-in-cheek nickname given to the far left–leaning city. The People's Republik was located at 878 Massachusetts Avenue in Cambridge.

Dive Bars and Sports Pubs

The story of modern Boston is a tale of two cities. On one hand, Boston is one of the priciest zip codes in the nation. Most of Boston's real estate is way out of the range for even most in the middle class. With high-paying jobs in the technology, science and business fields, Boston is a world-class city and one of the most desirable in the nation. The Boston area is home to Harvard University, the Massachusetts Institute of Technology and Boston College, among scores of other institutions of higher learning. Neighborhoods such as the Seaport District and the Fenway have been redeveloped exceptionally during the past fifteen years, leaving no trace of their gritty past.

At the same time that Boston continues to reinvent itself as a beacon of modern America, there is another side to Beantown that is rooted in tradition. This tradition is not of the Freedom Trail historic kind but of a city with working-class roots. Neighborhoods such as the North End and South Boston are still home to ethnic enclaves of hard-nosed folks with thick Boston accents, where the letter *r* is not in one's vocabulary, as in the classic "Pahk the cah in Hahvahd Yahd." This is the Boston of rabid sports fans who live and die with the Sox, the Cs, the Bs and the Pats. It is the neighborhoods with a local dive bar or watering hole where everyone actually knows your name. In this chapter, let's explore some of the best classic dive bars and watering holes in Boston. Expect the Sox on TV, a cold pitcher of Harpoon and soul-warming comfort food. Establishments including the L Street Tavern, the Lansdowne Pub and Sullivan's Tap are favorites for a bite and a cold beer on game day. Many of the places in this chapter are located either nearby Fenway Park and the TD Garden or are pillars of their neighborhoods (or both).

Somehow, it is comforting to know that modern Boston in the twenty-first century, full of heavily polished skyscrapers, tapas restaurants and gastropubs, still has neighborhood sports pubs, dive bars and eateries that are populated by locals and enthusiastic Boston sports fans. Just don't wear your Yankees cap!

THE WEST END

We are starting our tour of Boston-area sports pubs and dive bars in the West End. The West End was once a historic neighborhood, an area with brick residences that took up a third of the city's downtown core. From the mid-nineteenth century, this was historically an immigrant neighborhood. By the early twentieth century, a portion had fallen into disrepair. As part of the urban renewal movements that swept across many cities in the country during the mid-twentieth century, much of the old West End was demolished in the face of "progress." In turn, skyscraper residences and commercial buildings were erected. The West End and the city on the whole were forever changed.

Sullivan's Tap, 1934

One establishment that existed pre–wrecking ball West End is Sullivan's Tap. This no-frills dive and sports bar is located at 168 Canal Street in the shadow of the West End's best-known destination, the TD Garden. The TD Garden is the home court and ice of Boston's Celtics and Bruins, basketball and hockey teams, respectively. Sullivan's has poured cold ones since 1934. The bar is lined with sports memorabilia and is stocked with cheap beer. It has one of the longest bars in the city. In addition to pub grub and suds, Sully's includes pool tables and bar basketball hoops. It gets packed pre– and post–sports games. It is also a popular spot to watch Boston sports games on television. Recently, Sullivan's was acquired by the Greater Boston Bar Co., which also runs similar watering holes, such as the Beacon Hill Pub and the Tam.

The Greatest Bar, 2004

If Sullivan's represents the old school, the Greatest Bar is the new. Opened in 2004, the Greatest Bar features four floors of Boston history, sports, entertainment and politics, all wrapped into one building. The name "greatest" refers to a commemoration of all of the greatest events in Boston history. Each floor features a different theme, including the Greatest Room, with high-definition TVs and sports décor lining the walls. The second floor is a mezzanine overlooking the first floor, known as the Championship Room, which celebrates victories of the city's sports teams. Next, the Dirty Water Room highlights the accomplishments of Boston in the arts and media, including musicians, television shows and actors with Boston ties. Finally, on the fourth floor is the Boston Room, a wood-lined room featuring ties to Boston's political past, which includes large portraits of John Quincy Adams and John F. Kennedy. Also look for the Bruins-themed Penalty Box. Menu items include pizza, burgers and sandwiches. The Greatest Bar is located at 262 Friend Street.

THE FENWAY

Moving east through the city, the next sports bar destination is Lansdowne Street, bordering the north side of Fenway Park, home of the Boston Red Sox. It was once a seedy street teeming with nightclubs such as Mamma Kin and the Boston Tea Party and others located close by, such as the Rat in Kenmore Square. Today's Lansdowne Street in Kenmore Square is upscale, anchored by the Hotel Commonwealth and upscale restaurants. What were once independent music venues have been replaced with the House of Blues. Many of the establishments are operated by the Lyons Group, including the two that are mentioned here. Their properties vary in theme. Other holdouts include Cask 'n Flagon and Bill's Bar, which were located here long before the Red Sox and World Series Champions could be said in the same sentence (repeatedly). Brookline Avenue, close to Fenway, has been completely changed, with what were once warehouse-type buildings and parking lots having been transformed into high-rise luxury condos and chain restaurants and stores such as Target, Bar Louie and the Yard House.

Cask 'n Flagon, 1969

If one establishment has more direct ties to Fenway Park than any other, it has to be Cask 'n Flagon. The Cask, as it is known for short, has graced the outskirts of Fenway Park since 1969. On Fenway's outfield wall, there is even a small sign that points to the location of the Cask. Cask 'n Flagon is *the* place to hang out before and after Sox games. During game time, if you cannot make it into the ballpark, there are plenty of TVs from which to view the game. ESPN even gave Cask 'n Flagon the recognition of being the best baseball bar in the country. The food is crowd-pleasing fare, with burgers, short ribs, appetizers and salads, and at Cask there is also an extensive beer menu that features many local craft breweries, such as Harpoon, Mayflower and Canned Heat. At night, Cask also features a dance floor in the room next door, known as Oliver's. This name pays tribute to a rock club that was once there at which many big-name artists graced the stage, including Bruce Springsteen, Jimi Hendrix and Boston. Cask 'n Flagon is located at 62 Brookline Avenue, right across from Fenway Park. The building was originally a Ford dealership. There is a second Cask on Plain Street, Route 139, in Marshfield on the South Shore. It has the same great menu, beer selection and tribute to Boston sports without the city address.

Bleacher Bar, 2008

Looking into Fenway Park toward the Green Monster, it is easy to notice the large garage-style door located at the base of the centerfield bleachers. It is among the many intricacies of "American's best-loved (and oldest) ballpark." Bleacher Bar is located underneath the outfield bleachers but is accessible only from the sidewalk on the street. The food here is typical pub fare done well, but the real attraction is the view into the park. During game time, the bar gets understandably packed. Try and snag a seat or standing room to catch a glimpse of the game. Being literally inside Fenway Park, it is quite the feeling to watch a live baseball game while enjoying a menu item such as a burger or sandwich for lunch or more elaborate dishes, including salmon or short rib, for dinner. This was once a batting cage for the visiting team and was also used as a storage facility. The interior is wood-lined, accented by the unmistakable Fenway green. There is certainly more on this menu than the perfunctory Fenway Frank. The Bleacher Bar is located at 82A Lansdowne Street. Upon entering, walk down the steps to the field-level restaurant.

The Lansdowne, 2009

An establishment with the namesake of the street, located at 9 Lansdowne Street, this is an Irish pub that is a popular spot pre– and post–Red Sox games. It is a representative of the "new" Lansdowne, family friendly but still a pub that sports fans can be excited about. It has excellent food, with tacos and burgers on the menu (and even salads). It is a great place to watch a game on TV if you cannot grab a ticket or if the Sox are away. It has a wood-lined interior with chandeliers giving it a classy vibe. There is a branch of the Lansdowne at the Mohegan Sun casino in Uncasville, Connecticut.

NEIGHBORHOOD DIVES

Each neighborhood in Boston seems to have its local dive bar. From posh Beacon Hill to working-class Maverick Square in East Boston, each Boston 'hood has its watering hole. A whole book could be written on the dives of Boston. That being said, the focus for this title is going to be one of the most famous of them all.

L Street Tavern, 1962

L Street Tavern, located in South Boston, has become a bit of a Boston celebrity. Truly a corner bar, it is located at 658 East 8th Street at the corner of L Street in Southie. Located in a once rough-hewn area of the neighborhood, its iconic status was aided in part by the film *Good Will Hunting*. For those familiar with the 1997 Gus Van Sant film starring Ben Affleck and Matt Damon in their breakout roles, this was the bar where the neighborhood friends hung out and Damon's character, Will Hunting, met his future love interest, Minnie Driver's character, Skylar, for the first time.

L Street Tavern is an Irish pub but fits more under the category of dive and sports bars. With its celebrity status, L Street Tavern has been renovated. Its once divey exterior is now welcoming, with a painted brown façade. The interior is that of a comfortable neighborhood bar. Unlike Cheers, whose celebrity status turned the Bull & Finch Pub into a tourist must-visit, the L Street Tavern has remained a local spot. It is simply a classic bar with friendly staff and a regular clientele. It is easy to find the table where the *Good Will Hunting* crew hung out. It is covered with memorabilia from the film.

PART IV

CLASSIC BOSTON FOOD... AND WHERE TO FIND IT!

Notable Boston Dishes

OYSTERS

The briny bivalve was first publicly sold in America in 1763 at a basement saloon on Broad Street in New York City. During the nineteenth century, the oyster was so in vogue that oyster parlors, cellars and restaurants popped up in major cities and were often locations for political debate. As in the nineteenth century, in the twenty-first century, oysters are very much a popular menu item, especially in seaside Boston.

The most well-known oyster eatery is Union Oyster House, located at 41 Union Street in Boston. That location has been shucking away since 1826. Union Oyster House is known for its slew of celebrity diners, including John F. Kennedy, Bill Clinton and Meryl Streep. Statesman Daniel Webster would slurp down an average of six plates of half a dozen oysters a day, along with a tumbler of brandy and water.

Not with the same longevity as Union Oyster House, the Boston area is home to oyster farms such as the renowned Island Creek Oyster Company based out of Duxbury, Massachusetts. It owned the famous Island Creek Oyster Bar in Kenmore Square, which recently shuttered. Currently, it operates the Winsor House Inn and the seasonal outdoor Raw Bar at Island Creek, both in Duxbury.

Oysters vary in taste based on the ocean water's salinity, temperature and food consumed by the oyster. They can be found in the wild, but most of the oysters on menus today have been cultivated at oyster farms. Restaurants in the Boston area will serve raw oysters on the half shell based on location,

Oysters have always been on the menu at Union Oyster House. *Courtesy of Joseph Milano.*

such as locally from the seas of Duxbury, Plymouth or Wakefield, Rhode Island, or even as far away as off the coast of Washington and Oregon. Oysters are prepared in various ways, including the most popular raw on the half shell, fried or grilled. Oysters Rockefeller, baked with herbs, butter and breadcrumbs, can be found in Boston-area restaurants as appetizers but are more closely related to the southern United States. Oysters are a tasty way to consume essential minerals and vitamins, including calcium, selenium, vitamins A and B, zinc and iron.

CLAM CHOWDER

In New England, clam chowder can be found on seemingly every menu, from dive bar to five-star restaurant. Each establishment has its own take on the regional classic. In Boston, the New England clam chowder is king. This means the soup has a milk base. There are other variations of clam chowder as well, including the Rhode Island style, with clear broth, and Manhattan style, which has a tomato base. Personal preference rules here, but the most recognized as a clam chowder is the New England style.

In Boston, the New England style is the most ubiquitous, found on nearly every menu save for that of ethnic cuisines. In one way, clam chowder has become the gold standard, with bragging rights over whose chowder is the king of the city. Concocting a perfect chowder should be quite straightforward, although restaurants often put their own spin on the traditional recipe, which typically consists of milk, potatoes and onions, along with the clams, of course. A commonly added ingredient is bacon. Although the traditional chowder's ingredients are often consistent in most chowder houses, there are sometimes variations in thickness of the broth, as well as seasonings.

Clam chowder originated in Nova Scotia, and the word *chowder* is in reference to the kind of pot that is used to cook the soup. In the French language, the word for the cooking pot is *chaudiere*; in Latin, the word is *calderia*. The word's original use was in reference to the process of heating something up but became a term for the cooking vessel itself. The word *cauldron* is in reference to this Latin word. *Chowder* is derived from the Latin word, with its meaning used by the French in Nova Scotia. In this seafaring land, it was cod that first was included in the soup known as chowder.

It is easy to think of the word "chowder," especially in reference to clam chowder, as simply part of our vernacular, but pausing for a moment and reflecting on the word, it is quite niche. Most soups in a similar vein to chowder are referred to as soups or stews. A chowder is simply a fish soup from the Americas. Fish chowder and corn chowder—although corn is certainly not a fish—are also found on menus, but for the most part, clam chowder rules the kitchen.

Quite honestly, clam chowder's presence on menus throughout Boston is as common as Red Sox hats in Fenway Park on game day. There are so many worthy clam chowders steaming from the kitchens of Boston restaurants. Many of the classic restaurants already mentioned serve a fine cup of chowder, including the Barking Crab, Union Oyster House and Jasper White's Summer Shack.

For a true representative taste of New England clam chowder in Boston though, the one must-try is the chowder from Legal Sea Foods. This is truly iconic. Instead of loading the chowder with a bouillabaisse of ingredients, the recipe is quite simple but super tasty. With clams, potatoes, onions and herbs rounding out the major accent flavors of the chowder, it is not an elaborate recipe, but as is true in many cases, less is often more. Top it with oyster crackers, and this is a chowder that cannot be beat, as evidenced by the many awards that it has won.

BOSTON BAKED BEANS

Much has been said about Boston as "Beantown" and Boston baked beans. Even though the legume and the dish are often referred to as a Boston food, unlike clam chowder and lobster, it is not as easy to find it on menus of area restaurants. The bean for which Boston is known originated from a food used by the Indigenous people of the region that the colonists adapted for their own use. For the recipe of Boston baked beans, the dish is typically sweetened by molasses, an ingredient that the city was known for, which would eventually lead to vast wealth. Another major ingredient in Boston baked beans is bacon or salt pork.

As part of the Triangular Trade that shipped goods as well as slaves from the Americas to Europe and West Africa, molasses was imported into Boston. In Boston, molasses was used to make rum, which was then exported to West Africa. In West Africa, slaves were sent over to the West Indies to labor on sugar plantations. As this process continued, since Boston was an exporter of rum, the economy grew. On a side note, Boston is also known for the tragic Molasses Flood of 1919. A tank holding twelve thousand tons of molasses burst in the North End of the city. It injured 150 people, and 21 ended up perishing. Years later, on scorching summer days, the smell of molasses was still said to permeate the nostrils of those in the North End.

Boston baked beans was a popular dish to serve in New England. Still today, bean dinners are served at church halls in Yankee fashion, eating beans as a Saturday night meal. During days of strict Puritanical tradition of resting on the Sabbath, the meal was cooked on a Saturday and kept warm in the oven in a pot, as even cooking was prohibited on the Sabbath.

The nickname of "Beantown" has different origin stories. One story comes from the meal that sailors would consume in port in the city. As a quick meal, it was widely consumed as a fast food of sorts. Another story relates that the name stems from an Old Home Week celebration in the city during the summer of 1907. The sticker that was used as promotional material included beans in a traditional bean pot. The moniker stuck, and Boston's been Beantown ever since. During the 1880s, the team that was to be known as the Boston Braves (now the Atlanta Braves) was called the Boston Beaneaters; this version of the name's origin predates the Old Home Week story by decades.

There are numerous bean references in Boston, including the Beanpot ice hockey tournament, in which four college hockey teams—Boston University,

Boston College, Harvard University and Northeastern University—compete for the distinction of winning this local tournament.

For a true taste of Boston baked beans, make sure to order them as a side dish at Union Oyster House. Combine this with a cup of chowder, a dozen oysters, Boston scrod and a slice of Boston cream pie for dessert, and now you are "eating Boston"!

BOSTON CREAM PIE

With the word "Boston" in the name, this is one dessert with undeniable ties to the city. Heck, it is even the state dessert of Massachusetts! For a well-known after-dinner treat, it has a bit of controversy around it. For one, the Boston cream pie is certainly more cake than pie. It originated in the mid-1850s—some publications stating 1855 and others a year later—at the Parker House Hotel. French pastry chef Augustine François Anezin is credited with the original recipe. Other publications peg Chef Sanzian as the originator, with other sources crediting Chef Raelyn in the 1880s. Chef Anezin gets the nod from the Parker House as originator.

Even more controversy arises from the inspiration. One popular theory is that the Boston cream pie is derived from the Washington pie, which was a well-known cake with jelly filling in the 1800s. The pie reference also comes

A slice of Boston cream pie from Flour Bakery + Café. *Jaclyn Lamothe.*

from the fact that it was baked in a pan that was used for both pies and cakes. It was not included in a recipe book for many years, in part due to the fact that the cake, ahem, pie is quite complicated to make.

What cannot be argued is what the cake is made of. Typically, it is a sponge cake with chocolate icing on the top and filled with a cream or custard. Seeking a Boston cream pie in the city that bears its name should be quite easy. Popular versions hail from Italian bakeries such as Mike's and Modern Pastry. Well-regarded bakeries including Flour Bakery + Café are also known for their versions, as are classic restaurants such as Union Oyster House. The most sought after, though, is the original. Parker's Restaurant, located inside the Omni Parker Hotel, is best known for this dessert. The original has a different look than what is commonly thought of as Boston cream pie. Almond pieces line the outside of it, and lines of white chocolate are interwoven in the chocolate layer on top, creating a spiderweb appearance. Seek this out; it is truly decadent and delicious.

My favorite Boston cream pie can be found at the utterly delicious Boston establishment Flour Bakery + Café. Flour Bakery + Café is a mini-chain of bakeries, with nine outposts all in Boston or Cambridge, which began in the South End in the year 2000. The owner and head baker is Joanne Chang, who has become a Boston celebrity baker in her own right. Additionally, she is co-owner of the popular Myers + Chang, a modern Taiwanese restaurant that she operates with her partner, Christopher Myers. Back to the Boston cream pie though.

My conception of Boston cream pie in general is of a sticky texture and over-the-top sweet taste, resembling more of a Boston cream doughnut. For my personal palate, that is too sweet. At Flour, the Boston cream pie is perfect. Its design is more like a tiramisu with a distinct layering to it. The cream is light, with a sweet taste that is not overwhelming. The chocolate glaze that is drizzled on top drips down the sides, creating an attractive chocolate edging. The whole experience is still decadent without being excessive. Instead of a spiderweb design of vanilla on top of the chocolate, the design is more reminiscent of a leaf. With many locations scattered throughout Boston, as well as the original South End bakery located at 1595 Washington Street, Flour Bakery + Café is a must-visit, and while you are there, make sure to grab a piece of the Boston cream pie.

LOBSTER AND LOBSTER ROLLS

If any food is synonymous with the New England coast, it has to be lobster. In Boston, as the region's largest city, lobster makes a frequent appearance on menus of the city's restaurants. The lobster that is associated with the region goes by many nicknames, including the "American lobster," the "Boston lobster" and, most frequently, the "Maine lobster." Certainly, Maine is most associated with the tasty crustacean, with lobster fishing being one of the most prominent industries in the state. But the term "Maine lobster" is actually in reference to the Gulf of Maine, which spans past the state's coastlines, from Nova Scotia to the north and south to Cape Cod.

Visitors flock from far and wide for lobster in Boston. *Jaclyn Lamothe.*

The cold-water, hard-shell lobster is what locals and tourists alike flock to seafood restaurants all over New England for. This delicacy was once the opposite. During the time of the arrival of the Europeans to the shores of America, the sea was teeming with lobster. Indigenous peoples of the region included lobster in their diet but also used the shellfish as fertilizer. The lobster was wrapped in seaweed and put over warm rocks to cook, which was the inspiration for the ever-popular New England clambake. During the colonial period, lobster was seen as a pauper's protein source. Its ubiquitousness led to it being deemed food for the poor, servants and slaves. During the 1880s though, lobster had a newfound popularity and was found in the kitchens of New York and Boston.

The opposite of a poor man's food today, lobster is thought of as a luxury food, a delicacy. The prices can be steep when buying lobster by the pound. Nevertheless, it is a favorite food, especially on a warm New England summer day. Luckily, in Boston lobster can be found in restaurants all year long, prepared in a variety of ways. The steamed lobster dinner is the most popular preparation. The lobster roll has risen in popularity to challenge the steamed lobster in terms of the favorite way to enjoy it. Other dishes include baked

Lobster rolls are a popular alternative to steamed lobsters. *Jaclyn Lamothe.*

stuffed lobster; lobster Thermidor, a French creamy stuffed lobster dish; lobster macaroni and cheese; lobster grilled cheese; and lobster over pasta. It can be prepared and cooked in almost any way. Similar to clam chowder, lobster can be found in many of Boston's restaurants, from a takeout stand such as Sullivan's at Castle Island to fine dining at Neptune Oyster, from urban seafood shacks like the Barking Crab to old-school favorites such as the Union Oyster House.

The process of preparing to eat lobster can be an arduous task. The cracking of the shells, fishing out the smaller pieces of meat of the knuckles and removing the tail from the body is too much for some lobster lovers. For this reason, a lobster roll is an understandable alternative to the steamed lobster. Lobster rolls are typically served on a buttered bun and are full of delicious lobster meat. There are two schools of lobster roll: the Maine style and the Connecticut style. The Maine variation is more well known. Cold but fresh lobster meat is served on a bun, highlighted with mayonnaise and possibly some celery or a leaf of lettuce. The Connecticut version is served hot. The meat itself is warm, placed on a buttery toasted roll and served fresh. My personal preference is the Connecticut version. Nothing beats a warm lobster roll. Also, lobster salad rolls can be found on area menus, a cold, mayo-doused version on lettuce (with more mayonnaise than found on the cold Maine version).

The hot lobster roll is hard to find outside of the Constitution State. This being said, many of the lobster rolls found in Boston and environs are Maine lobster rolls, with the lobster served cold with a touch of mayo.

Green Harbor Lobster Pound

For the coastal towns on the South Shore of Boston, lobstering is a primary occupation. Scituate, Plymouth and Marshfield are among the busiest lobstering communities in the region. Due to this reason, almost every town has its own lobster pound. Weymouth, Hingham, Cohasset, Marshfield (Green Harbor) and Plymouth (Manomet) are among the towns with lobster

The Green Harbor Lobster Pound in Marshfield is a summer tradition. *Jaclyn Lamothe.*

pounds. In pursuit of the South Shore's best lobster roll, the place that gets mentioned the most is the Green Harbor Lobster Pound.

The Green Harbor Lobster Pound is literally tucked away in the residential beachside neighborhood of Green Harbor in Marshfield. This is a no-frills seafood stand that is only open from Memorial Day through Labor Day. Picnic table dining outside or taking it to go are the only options. The focal point of the menu is, of course, the lobster, and the stand is known far and wide for its lobster rolls. They come in two sizes, regular and jumbo. Although the price tag is steep for the jumbo, there is plenty of meat in it to split it with a friend. It is served simply on a buttered bun. The meat is cold, but in this case, it does not matter; the freshness is unparalleled.

The waterfront view is authentic. This is clearly not a tourist destination. The experience of sitting at one of the handful of picnic tables on the cove and chowing down on a lobster roll is perfection. Another must-try menu item is the onion rings. They are thin, shoestring onion rings that are lightly battered and truly amazing. The Green Harbor Lobster Pound is located at 131 Beach Street in Marshfield.

James Hook Lobster

Since 1925, James Hook Lobster and Company has been Boston's place for fresh lobsters. Located at 440 Atlantic Avenue close to the Fort Point Channel and across from the Barking Crab, it is known far and wide as a crustacean destination. At James Hook, both lobsters and lobster rolls are popular items. In 2008, James Hook was dealt a serious blow when it caught fire, destroying the iconic brown building with large, seemingly handwritten white letters reading "James Hook + Co." Thirty tons of lobster was lost in the blaze. Luckily, the building was rebuilt and is once again a staple of the Boston waterfront, with the name again scrawled on the harbor-facing side of the building.

James Hook Lobster is a lobster shack inside the city. *Author's photo.*

The lobster company is owned by the third generation of the Hook family, brothers Jimmy, Eddie and Al. The lobster pound looks out of place in twenty-first-century Boston, especially with the high-rises of the Seaport District and the Financial District surrounding it. Since being rebuilt, it would look more natural on the coast of Maine than in the heart of modern downtown Boston. The fire has not been the only thing to threaten James Hook. The Great Depression, the Big Dig and plans for a lavish new hotel to be built on the spot have put the little lobster pound that could on the endangered list. Even with the ever-changing city, what does not change is the fact that locals and tourists alike have a hankering for lobster that James Hook fills. For a taste of Maine lobster by way of Boston, James Hook and Company ships anywhere within the continental United States.

Neptune Oyster

Since 2004, Neptune Oyster in the North End has become a favorite for seafood in the city of Boston. Heralded as Boston's best restaurant and best oyster bar by different publications, Neptune Oyster is most known for its lobster roll. For those who argue about the variations of lobster roll, Neptune serves it both cold with mayonnaise and warm with butter, making folks from both Connecticut and Maine happy. It is located at 63 Salem Street.

JORDAN MARSH BLUEBERRY MUFFINS

Jordan Marsh was a large department store that covered a whole city block in Downtown Crossing. The store had its roots beginning in 1841 and closed up shop in the mid-1990s when it was acquired by Macy's. In addition to its flagship Boston store, Jordan Marsh branched out with offshoot stores in area malls such as Braintree, Burlington and Peabody, as well as farther out in the nation, including Miami and San Diego. You may wonder why a department store is written about in a book about classic Boston restaurants. It is because Jordan Marsh served iconic blueberry muffins, gigantic in size and full of blueberries. The smell and the taste of these muffins were part of the treat of visiting Jordan Marsh.

Although Jordan Marsh became Macy's, where the blueberry muffins ceased along with the name change, the muffins have returned. At Jordan's Furniture, a Boston-area furniture store chain, the muffins can be found at the location in Avon, Massachusetts, during Christmastime. Those who have had both say that these are just as good as the original.

The blueberry muffins are not the only throwback from Jordan Marsh that Jordan's Furniture acquired. From the 1940s to 1972 and then from 1990 until closure, Jordan Marsh in downtown Boston was the site of the Enchanted Village, an animatronic holiday display of Victorian Christmas scenes. It was a tradition each December at Jordan Marsh, along with visits with Santa. Enchanted Village moved to the Boston City Hall Plaza during the early 2000s and eventually to the Hynes Convention Center. In 2009, Jordan's Furniture bought the holiday décor and completely refurbished it. It has been located at the Avon store ever since, along with visits with Santa and the distinctive Jordan Marsh blueberry muffins. And believe it or not, the two "Jordan" monikers are not related.

CANNOLI

Another food item closely associated with the city is cannoli. Although not an indigenous food such as lobster or oysters, nor a staple such as Boston baked beans or scrod, cannoli, arriving with Italian immigrants, is a mainstay dessert. Of course, where better to find cannoli than in Boston's North End, the city's Italian enclave. Bakeries throughout the city and its environs serve cannoli, but the most popular have to be from the Big

Three of the North End's bakeries: Mike's Pastry, Modern Pastry and Bova's Bakery. Locals and tourists may argue over which is the cannoli king. The most well known of the three is Mike's Pastry, whose cannoli is significantly larger. The fried cannoli shell is filled with a semi-sweet ricotta filling. Dusted with powdered sugar and topped with chocolate chips, varieties at these bakeries run the gamut from conventional to truly unique. For a detailed description of these bakeries' cannoli, see the chapter on the North End.

Cannoli from Bova's Bakery, Mike's and Modern Pastry. *Jaclyn Lamothe.*

SCROD

The fish that is most closely associated with Boston is not actually a species of fish at all, and that is scrod. Scrod is a generic term for a whitefish, including a juvenile cod or a haddock. For a fanciful species, the etymology of the word is more rooted in fiction than fact, which is perfect for a fish of no absolute genus. One legend of the scrod closely associated with Boston is that the term began at Parker's Restaurant. Granted, this dish has been a mainstay on the menu and continues there today. Notable about the Parker House's scrod is that the fish is the freshest, from the top of the pile of the fishermen's catch at the wharves of Boston. The fish at the top were always the last caught, making it the freshest and the most desirable for restaurateurs to serve. The dish is often served baked, as it is at Parker's Restaurant, where it is listed as "schrod." At Legal Sea Foods, one of the most popular dishes is Anna's Boston Baked Scrod. Union Oyster House's boiled fresh Boston scrod is a fan favorite as well. Many restaurants serve scrod as their "catch of the day" or the freshest white fish. The fish is so closely associated with the city that even at restaurants outside Boston, it is often referred to as "Boston scrod" on the menu.

PART V

JUST-OUT-OF-TOWN CLASSICS

A Trip Out of Town

As Boston is related to certain foods—such as chowder, Boston cream pie and Boston baked beans, to name a few—so are its suburbs. Instead of a town having a specific cuisine, whole regions around Boston are known for different foods. From the North Shore to the South Shore, although close geographically to the city, they each have dishes that are location specific.

The North Shore is anchored by Gloucester, a historic working-class fishing town that drew national attention with Sebastian Junger's book *The Perfect Storm*, which was then turned into a blockbuster movie of the same name starring George Clooney and Mark Wahlberg. Quaint towns and villages such as Rockport, Magnolia, Ipswich and Manchester-by-the-Sea turn the North Shore into popular touristy spots, with picturesque seaside communities. The region is also known for Salem, which of course earned its notoriety through the tragic witch trials in the late 1600s. In the present day, Salem has become an ever-popular tourist destination, in large part due to its witchy connections. Other towns north of Boston, such as Saugus, Melrose and Stoughton, were working-class communities that, with the growth of Boston, have increased in popularity and wealth.

Starting our journey, this region is known for two major food items: fried clams and roast beef sandwiches. Given the proximity to the ocean, the fried clams may seem like an obvious choice, but did you know that Woodman's in Essex, Massachusetts, claims to be the originator of the fried clam? Although that location is still the most popular in the region, if not one of the most popular in the whole country, other contenders to the fried clam crown include J.T. Farnham's and the Clam Box.

Roast beef may come as a surprise since beef is more synonymous with the cattle-heavy Midwest. The towns just north of Boston, including Revere, Lynn and Beverly, are all known for their fast-food specialty, the roast beef sandwich. It's served simply—thinly sliced, tender roast beef on a poppy seed bun or onion roll punctuated by mayonnaise and barbecue sauce. The most well-known of the North Shore roast beef joints is Kelly's, with the original seaside location on Revere Beach.

Also north of the city, and not associated with a distinct menu item but still food-centric with a slew of classic restaurants, is Route 1. The Route 1 corridor from Saugus to Peabody transports the driver back to the 1950s and 1960s. If any place abides by the adage "bigger is better," it is Route 1. That mantra is illustrated by Prince Pizzeria, which includes a few-stories-tall Leaning Tower of Pisa perched atop the Italian eatery, and Kowloon, a humongous Polynesian-themed Chinese restaurant.

My first trip on this iconic road happened in 2002. Back then, there were more traces of mid-twentieth-century nostalgia than there are currently. As Boston's desirability has grown, these suburbs have been transformed into upper-class bedroom towns. With it, condos, chain stores and restaurants have replaced much of the old Route 1. Some pieces of the past, such as the gigantic cactus that used to mark the location of the Hilltop Steakhouse, still stand. The huge cactus now marks a residential and commercial plaza. The dinosaur-themed mini-golf, when just entering Saugus, is also gone, but the orange tyrannosaurus rex is a beacon of the past and greets visitors to another commercial plaza. This strip of road at one time held the largest number of restaurants, which in turn had the capacity to entertain the most diners anywhere in the United States. Restaurants that are big in size still make their mark on Route 1. Others, including McDonald's, have larger-than-usual road signs. Little by little, "progress" gobbles up the remnants of the road, such as the demolition of the Ship Restaurants and plaza, which included a replica life-size boat for the restaurant, but the lighthouse still flanks the other side. The roadside motels such as the Fern Motel, which advertised on its sign that it had color TV, met their fate by the wrecking ball in recent years.

This adventure also takes us to MetroWest, the suburban region west of the city. The most iconic restaurant in this area is Ken's Steakhouse. Not only does this restaurant have a decades-long history, but it is also associated with the famous salad dressing, a top seller in the nation.

The final stop just out of town is the South Shore. This region is anchored by the historic community of Plymouth, the landing place of the Pilgrims and the first established permanent English settlement in New England. The South Shore of course is known for its seafood. Seaside towns, including Plymouth, Quincy and Marshfield, house some of the best seafood shacks and restaurants in the state and are also known for a certain type of pizza. South Shore bar pizza is truly different and utterly delicious. It is typically served in a personal pan size, and the cheese used is cheddar, not mozzarella. The crispiness of the pizza gives it a crunch, but the pizza is never burned. Although it is associated with the South Shore, much of the best pizza actually comes from the area just south of the city, with establishments such as the Lynwood Café in Randolph and Town Spa Pizza in Stoughton. Closer to the sea, the Black Raspberry Pub in Plymouth and Poopsie's in Pembroke are all regional favorites.

Clearly, from the North Shore to the South Shore, classic Boston restaurants branch out way beyond city lines, creating classic Boston-area restaurants.

The North Shore

WOODMAN'S OF ESSEX, 1914

Fried clams seem like they have been around forever. Not many people stop to think about where the crunchy fried bivalve originated. Woodman's of Essex, located at 121 Main Street in Essex (Route 133), is the originator of the fried clam. The story goes that Woodman's began as a small store selling groceries, clams that were hand dug and potato chips that owner Lawrence "Chubby" Woodman made. Chubby and his wife Bessie's fortunes turned around after a twist of fate. One customer, a Mr. Tarr, facetiously suggested that Woodman fry a few of his clams since the business was less than booming. The first clams were fried on July 3, 1916. A day later, on the Fourth of July, they were served and became a big hit. Thus, the fried clam was born.

Fast-forward over one hundred years, and Woodman's is one of the most famous and highly praised seafood shacks in the country. The restaurant is still in the family, with Steve Woodman (grandson of Chubby and Bessie) as the current owner. The fried clams have been lauded by varied publications, including *Vogue*, *Zagat*, *Forbes* and the *Boston Globe*. The clams are perfect golden morsels, a combination of the crunchiness of the batter with the sweetness of the whole belly. Of course, there is much more on the menu than just fried clams. Lobster is always a popular choice. One menu item that gets rave reviews at Woodman's and cannot be found at many other restaurants is the fried lobster tail. If lobster is not delicious enough on its own, try it battered, fried and then dunked in butter!

Fried clams! *Author's photo.*

Order at the counter, grab a table, wait for your name to be called and chow down. There is booth seating inside and picnic tables outside. The restaurant is spacious, but during the summer months, expect a long line at Woodman's. The geographic area that surrounds Woodman's, both behind it and across the street, is the Essex River tidal flats. This marshy area is home to the bounty of the sand that has put the area's seafood shacks on the culinary map.

Woodman's is not the only mainstay fried clam restaurant in this region. The other two that make up the trifecta include J.T. Farnham's, also just down the street in Essex, and the Clam Box in nearby Ipswich. One reason that the clams are so tasty in this region is due to their freshness, pulling them right out of the sandy shore. Roads sometimes have nicknames based on commodities found nearby. In this case, Route 133 from Ipswich to Essex should be nicknamed the "fried clam highway," with all three iconic clam shacks located on this same road.

THE CLAM BOX, 1935

For a restaurant specializing in fried clams, there is no better architecture than that of the Clam Box in Ipswich. The building is literally shaped like a cardboard clam box. Near the top of the building, the sides flank outward, reminiscent of an open clam box. The Clam Box originates from 1935 and has been owned by the Aggelakis family since the 1980s. Matron and owner Chickie Aggelakis passed away in the summer of 2020. The Clam Box is located at 246 High Street in Ipswich, on Route 133, fried clam highway. The Clam Box is also known for other delectable seafood, much of it in the fried variety. Lobster rolls are very popular here as well. The fried clams used at the Clam Box are large. There is seating both indoors and out. One word of note: even in the busiest of rush times, which on the weekends in the summer can mean quite the wait, the staff changes the oil used for frying mid-afternoon at 2:30 p.m. At 2:30, the cooking operation ceases while the oil is refreshed. With the oil being changed twice a day, the Clam Box makes certain the fried seafood is utmost in quality.

J.T. FARNHAM'S, 1941

Farnham's, which opened in 1941, is the "newest" of the big three fried clam destinations. It is also located on Route 133, at 88 Eastern Avenue in Essex, just down the street from Woodman's. This fried clam and seafood lover's dream is situated on the same marshland of the Essex River. Quite honestly it is a toss-up who serves the best fried clams of these three. Of course, everyone has their own favorite. Tourists seem to be more familiar with Woodman's and the Clam Box than Farnham's. This could mean that if you are looking for your fried clam fix on a warm summer afternoon, Farnham's might have less of a line than the other two.

That being said, Farnham's is popular in its own right. Even though it may not be quite as well known, this does not mean it is any less tasty. Point-blank, their seafood is delicious. The bivalves they use for their fried clams are Ipswich clams. From the outside, the sign at Farnham's reads "Famous Clams." These beauties are crispy and sweet. They also serve a great chowder. Not just clam chowder at Farnham's though; they serve an array, including New England clam chowder, Nana's haddock chowder, spicy Manhattan chowder and clish, which is part clam and part fish chowder. The most heralded though is the seafood chowder, which includes a bouillabaisse of delectable seafood containing clams, scallops, haddock, shrimp and lobster. What a combination! Make sure to try other top choices, such as the fried oysters and fish tacos, which are rarely found on the menus of New England seafood shacks. At Farnham's, they even make their own tartar sauce.

Farnham's began its life as Wilson's Fried Clams, operated by the namesake family. The restaurant was bought by Joseph and Matilda Farnham, who changed the name to reflect their surname. In 1994, "J.T." was added to "Farnham's" because Joseph and Terry Cellucci bought the clam shack. They kept the name, which was widely known, but added a recognition to themselves with the "J and T" for "Joseph and Terry." Put in your order, grab a picnic table, get your food and enjoy the perfect view of the Essex salt marsh behind Farnham's while noshing on some truly awesome fried clams.

THE ROAST BEEF SANDWICH

If fried clams are the North Shore staple that drives tourists there—or that tourists drive there for—the dish that keeps the locals happy is the roast beef sandwich. Now, for the uninitiated, the roast beef sandwich

A classic North Shore roast beef sandwich from Kelly's Roast Beef. *Jaclyn Lamothe.*

sounds like a mundane menu item that can be found at delis from coast to coast. Often this meat is served too well done, making it a dry sandwich. On the North Shore, this is certainly not the case. The meat is so tender and moist, cooked rare, giving the meat pile a pink hue. On the North Shore, the argument rages as to who serves the best roast beef. Most towns in each community house at least one of these establishments. Most are no-frills, old-fashioned places, often housed in strip malls or on busy roads. Among the most famous are Nick's Famous, Harrison's, Beachmont, Billy's Roast Beef and Seafood, King's, Miko's, Zeno's, Supreme, Bill and Bob's, Mino's, Royal Land 'n Sea, Mike's and Kelly's. Kelly's is where it all started. Some diners and other restaurants criticize Kelly's for "selling out" since they have a few locations throughout the North Shore (and had opened up other branches, including inside a Jordan's Furniture store and in the Allston neighborhood of Boston, both of which have since closed). The North Shore–style roast beef is so popular that it has spread beyond the confines of this region, spilling over into New Hampshire at places such as the highly regarded Blue House and on the South Shore at Brother's and Angelo's. What these places have in common is their simple names and their dedication to the roast beef sandwich. The term "three-way" is used to describe what many feel is the best preparation of the sandwich. In addition to the meat and bun, it is served with cheese (typically generic American cheese), mayonnaise and barbecue sauce. The barbecue sauce of choice is often James River barbecue sauce. The bun is most often baked by another North Shore institution, Malden's Piantedosi Baking Company. The typical three sizes that are served include the junior, regular and the Super Beef, which is the North Shore way of saying "large." The smaller sizes are often served on a sesame seed bun, but the Super Beef piles its way onto an onion roll. Other condiments and toppings can be added to the roast beef sandwich, including lettuce, tomato, pickles and horseradish mayonnaise.

Kelly's Roast Beef, 1951

One would think that the roast beef sandwich would originate in a cattle-rich region of the country such as Colorado or Kansas, not the North Shore of Massachusetts. Kelly's is the original roast beef restaurant, where legend says the roast beef sandwich was born in 1951. Kelly's has a few locations, but the original in Revere—at 410 Revere Beach Boulevard right across from Revere Beach—serves fried seafood and other food but is best known for the roast beef sandwich. It all began as a bit of an accident. Original owners Frank V. McCarthy and Raymond Carey manned a hot dog stand at Revere Beach. There was leftover roast beef from a wedding that took place at the

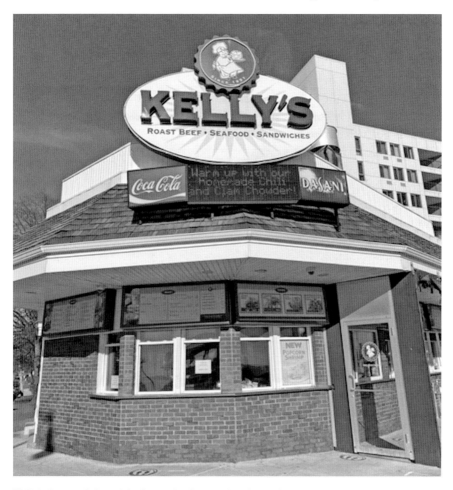

Kelly's, home of the original roast beef sandwich. *Jaclyn Lamothe.*

Paul Roger House, which was owned by Carey's family. The meat was sliced, placed on buns and sold at the hot dog stand, making it the maiden voyage of the roast beef sandwich. It was a hit, and the establishment of Kelly's as a roast beef mecca was born. Clearly, neither McCarthy's nor Carey's first or last name is Kelly, so how did the restaurant come to have that name? It is actually named after Tom Kelly, a friend of theirs.

The Revere Beach Kelly's is still just a walk-up stand. Look for the iconic neon green sign marking its location. At Kelly's, the sirloin has been aged for twenty-five days, and each sandwich is made to order. Even though there are four locations—Revere, Saugus, Danvers and Medford—the roast beef is roasted at each restaurant individually, not at one central location and then shipped over. The director of operations is Dan Doherty, who has been with Kelly's since he was in high school in the 1970s. The original Kelly's is located in Revere. Unlike most of the other roast beef joints in the North Shore, Kelly's roast beef is not served rare. The beef is brown, not pink. No matter what though, the roast beef sandwich at Kelly's is so tender. Order a "three way," with the roast beef on a Pantedosi's roll (onion roll for the large) with American cheese, James River barbecue sauce and mayonnaise. The James River sauce, which is a North Shore mainstay even though it is from Virginia, is the perfect condiment since it has a bit of a horseradish kick to it, giving the sandwich an extra bite without it being overwhelming.

TO ELABORATE ON EVERY CLASSIC roast beef sandwich restaurant in the North Shore clearly would lead to its own book just on this topic—and quite a few extra pounds for its author. Practically all of the restaurants have their own cult following, with locals proclaiming that their favorite is the obvious choice as number one. A documentary has even been filmed about the North Shore roast beef craze.

Restaurant Row: Route 1 from Saugus to Peabody

Americana at Its Finest

North of Boston, Route 1 between the towns of Saugus and Peabody was known for having the largest number of restaurants per mile while serving the largest number of diners in the whole country, giving it the nickname "Restaurant Row." Massive Hilltop Steakhouse could accommodate 1,300 diners at one time, and Kowloon, which bills itself as "America's largest Asian dining complex," can fit 1,200 customers under its roof. Although the 1950s kitsch is not as present today as it was years ago, Route 1's bygone flavor is retained.

At one time, in addition to Kowloon and Hilltop, hungry travelers could choose other roadside attractions and behemoth restaurants, including the Ship Restaurant, which was styled like an actual ship; Prince Pizzeria; and Weylu's, a replica of Forbidden City. Only Kowloon and Prince's remain currently. The fates of the other three have been determined by the wrecking ball. Once upon a time, motels such as Ferns, North Side and Avalon, advertising air conditioning or color TV, dotted the landscape of Route 1. Some still exist, although they are being routed out by modern hotels springing up in their place. Mini golf styled with large reptiles of the Jurassic age or grazing plastic cows outside Hilltop Steakhouse was to be expected on Route 1. Although the times have changed on this road, the past is still present, with even newer eateries such as Polcari's (part of the Regina Pizzeria family) and Santarpio's occupying mega restaurant space.

Although Hilltop Steakhouse is gone, the sixty-eight-foot cactus remains. It now advertises the Avalon apartment complex and newer restaurants

This giant cactus was once the sign for the Hilltop Steakhouse, an example of the larger-than-life architecture of Route 1. *Jaclyn Lamothe.*

such as 110 Grill that are located in its place. The cows are gone though. At one time, Hilltop Steakhouse, which thrived for fifty-two years in that location, could feed busloads. It was a popular dining destination for out-of-towners and certainly appealed to locals as well. It was owned by butcher Frank Giuffrida, whose name was in script on the sign. Other branches of

173

Hilltop existed as well in the towns of Braintree, Springfield and Hartford, Connecticut, but Saugus was the headquarters. At one time, this was the largest restaurant in the country. The statistics of how much of certain products the Hilltop went through in a week are staggering. For example, in its prime, Hilltop served 20,500 pounds of beef in a week!

Another imposing structure perched atop a hill close to the southern section of the commercial strip of Route 1 was Weylu's. It looked like a temple, patterned after the Forbidden City in China, but was actually a humongous Chinese restaurant. It only lasted for ten years, from 1989 to 1999, under the banner of Weylu's. Afterward, it opened sporadically under different ownership for the next ten years. It became vacant in 2009 and was demolished a few years after.

KOWLOON, 1950

Located here since 1950, the dining destination for many travelers on Route 1 is Kowloon. Kowloon is a multi-cuisine Asian foods restaurant where Chinese, Szechuan, Cantonese, Thai, Polynesian and Japanese cuisines are all served, with around three hundred items on the menu. Expect an exciting experience at the largest Asian dining complex in America.

Kowloon began as the Mandarin House, a restaurant serving Chinese and American food owned by the grandparents of the current Kowloon generation. The small twenty-four-seat restaurant was an ice cream parlor prior to its use as the Mandarin House. In 1958, Bill and Madeline Wong bought the restaurant from Madeline's parents and changed the name to Kowloon after an area of Hong Kong. The restaurant business was also in Bill's family, as his parents, Goe Shing and Lem Ding, ran Mai Fong, a restaurant in Boston. In a fifty-year span, the Wongs renovated and expanded Kowloon with five additions. The giant restaurant is able to accommodate 1,200 customers. Diners can enjoy a large variety of dishes in different themed rooms, including the Volcano Bay Room, which includes a fountain in the middle; the Tiki Lagoon; the Mandarin Room; the Thai Grille; and the Hong Kong Lounge. The Luau Room is used for functions and doubles as a comedy club in which top entertainers have performed, including a pre-*Seinfeld* Jerry Seinfeld, Phyllis Diller and musical acts such as the Temptations.

Currently, Kowloon's owners are the third generation, including Bob, Stanley, Donald, Andy, Linda and Lisa, with the fourth generation also working there. In addition, Donald Wong is a state representative. Kowloon employs around two hundred people and is known to serve one thousand pu pu platters in a week. Kowloon even has its own gift shop, selling tiki mugs similar to the décor inside the restaurant, as well as T-shirts and stuffed animals. It is the hangout for Boston sports stars, with many of their pictures plastered on the wall. In 2001, Madeline and Bill cemented their legacy by being named to the Massachusetts Hospitality Hall of Fame. Among the encyclopedic menu, some of the most popular options include the iconic Saugus Wings, slathered in a special concoction that will never be revealed outside the Wong family, and the Fancy Chicken, which is served in a pineapple shell. Kowloon represents the old, larger-than-life legacy of Route 1 that is still vibrant in the twenty-first century. It is as popular today as it has ever been.

PRINCE PIZZERIA, 1961

Among the more head-turning (and hopefully not accident-inducing) structures on Route 1 is the replica of the Leaning Tower of Pisa. Prince Pizzeria, owned and operated by the Castraberti family, has been slightly leaning since 1961. It proclaims itself as the "largest family-owned pizzeria" in the country. The restaurant's first owner was World War II veteran Arthur Castraberti. Castraberti worked for the Prince Macaroni Company nearby.

The leaning tower of Prince Pizzeria. *Jaclyn Lamothe.*

At that time, the pizzeria was just a small drive-in restaurant. The company wanted to transfer Castraberti to Canada, but he inquired about the status of the drive-in pizzeria, which was also owned by Prince. Prince made a deal with him. If he could erase the substantial debt that the company had incurred over the years of its operation within ten years, the restaurant would be his. Of course, the rest is history. Prince Pizzeria was in the hands of Castraberti and has been packing the house ever since. The restaurant can accommodate seven hundred guests and also contains a comedy club with performers including Lenny Clarke, Jimmie "JJ" Walker and Christine Hurley gracing the stage. The restaurant is still owned by the Castraberti family and is popular for its Italian dishes, including the lasagna, spaghetti and, of course, pizza. The pizza is often heralded as one of the top pies in the region. It is located at 517 Broadway in Saugus.

LUCKILY FOR DINERS, ROUTE 1 still has traces of its past with large restaurants that seat hundreds cooking absolutely delicious food.

The South Shore

BAR PIZZA

From Neapolitan to flatbreads, from Greek style to brick oven–fired, pizza comes in many and varied forms throughout the Boston area. The number one unique style for pizza is the bar pizza. Although it is synonymous with the South Shore, some of the most popular spots for bar pizza are in Brockton, Randolph and Canton. It is generally more of a south-of-Boston specialty.

Bar pizza is served in a small personalized pan that it is cooked in, about ten inches in diameter. It's a classic dish found mainly in area restaurants, bars and taverns. It is the specialty of no-frills, old-school joints and is often accompanied by a pitcher of domestic beer. The traditional bar pizza is a cheese pizza, and instead of mozzarella, most bar pizza joints use cheddar. Another key to the bar pizza is the crust, which has a great crunch to it. A secret is to order the pizza "extra crispy." And remember, it's crispy, certainly not burned!

Bar pizza can be found in a variety of establishments throughout the south of Boston. Cape Cod Café in Brockton is among the earliest and most popular. Established by the Jamoulis family over seventy years ago, it now has expanded to five branches, but the Brockton location is the original and has the classic old-school vibe. Another popular bar pizza place is Lynwood Café in Randolph, which has been open since 1949 and fits the bill as an old-school establishment. It has pinball games to play while waiting for your pizza and beer. Town Spa Pizza in Stoughton has existed for over sixty

The bar pizza, a South Shore staple. This pizza is from the Black Raspberry Pub in Plymouth. *Jaclyn Lamothe.*

years and is known for its bar pizza. Younger than these, but another classic, is Poopsie's in Pembroke, which has sat in the same strip mall on Route 139 since 1973. It's the kind of place where getting a table in the evening, especially during the weekend, is difficult since it is always packed. Poopsie's is dark inside, with wooden chairs placed around wooden tables, situated close together. It's definitely like entering the 1970s; all that is missing is the cigarette smoke. D'Ann's in Abington, another popular spot for bar pizza, has been open since 1959.

Not every classic bar pizza spot has to be old; Damien's Pub in Hanson has been open since 1998 and is renowned for its take on bar pizza. Not every bar pizza place has to be divey either. Take West End Grill, which opened in Kingston (also with a location in Randolph) in 2018. The tables are draped in actual tablecloths, and the restaurant features a well-chosen craft beer selection. The bar pizza holds up to the rest.

Although bar pizza is typically associated with a plain cheese pizza, there are many exotic takes on the dish that are really good. These include the BLT pizza served at Damien's Pub; the Greek pizza with olives, feta, cheddar and spinach at the Black Raspberry Pub in Plymouth; and the chicken bacon ranch pizza at Squinny's, also in Plymouth.

MetroWest

KEN'S STEAKHOUSE, 1941

The area of the MetroWest is the title given to describe towns that are west of Boston but east of Worcester, which is the second-largest city in New England. These include Framingham, Natick, Wayland and many other cities and towns in this region. Unlike other regions just outside the city, MetroWest does not have one particular cuisine associated with it, like bar pizza in the South Shore or fried clams and roast beef in the North Shore. "Classic Restaurants of MetroWest" could certainly be a title of its own, but one restaurant in particular stands out for posterity that needs to be included in this title, and that is Ken's Steakhouse in Framingham.

After only a few years in the restaurant industry, husband-and-wife team of Ken and Florence Hanna purchased a small diner on Route 9 in Framingham (at that time devoid of eating establishments) and eventually turned it into a highly successful endeavor. In 1935, in the midst of the Great Depression, the Hannas opened Lakeside Café in nearby Natick. It was across from the shores of Lake Cochituate, a popular recreation spot that was formerly a reservoir for the city of Boston. While there, the Hannas began to attract a following at their small restaurant. People loved the food and appreciated the familial hospitality. After five years at the Lakeside Café and one year at the Sandy Burr Country Club in Wayland, the Hannas purchased the former McHale's Diner and began anew at this location with Café 41.

Ken Hanna had made a name for himself at his previous dining establishments, so upon the opening of Café 41, fans of his food flocked there. Although the name was Café 41, many individuals referred to it as "Ken's." Eventually, the name was changed to what it is still called today.

Ken's Steakhouse began as a small restaurant where customers could enjoy a delicious meal that would not break the bank. Along with the regulars from his Natick days, word of mouth spread about the Hannas' new restaurant in Framingham. Even though the location has stayed the same since 1941, it has been dramatically expanded. In 1945, the Lamp Post Room was added, followed by the Hickory Room in 1957, along with the lounge being updated. Café V was added in 1959, creating a vast complex.

Ken's historically and currently is known for its cuts of beef. Prime sirloin, prime rib and filet mignon are popular menu items. Ken's also includes seafood and pasta on the menu. Beef is so popular at Ken's that a child-size filet mignon is even included on the children's menu. The classic Boston meal of scrod is one of the most sought-after seafood dishes at Ken's.

Ken's Steakhouse continues to be a top dining destination in Greater Boston even eighty years after its establishment. It is known far and wide for its top cuts of beef. In addition to being a meat lover's dream, Ken's is even more famous for its salads, in particular, the dressing. Ken's Steakhouse is owned and operated by Timothy and Darlene Hanna. It is located at 95 Worcester Road (Route 9) in Framingham.

Ken's Salad Dressing

The Italian salad dressing served at Ken's Steakhouse was such a hit that numerous customers wished it were bottled to take home. In 1958, it happened. Friends of the Hannas, Frank and Louise Crowley, took the salad dressing recipes and started bottling Ken's salad dressing. Over sixty years later, Ken's salad dressing is the third most popular dressing on the market. With over four hundred products made by Ken's Foods (including the acquisition of Sweet Baby Ray's barbecue sauce in 2005), Ken's dressings, marinades and sauces are in most American refrigerators.

Ken's dressing is no longer made in the Crowleys' kitchen. The headquarters is located farther west down Route 9 in the town of Marlborough. They also have plants throughout the country, including in Las Vegas, Georgia and Indiana. The Italian dressing is what started it all, but Ken's now comes in sixty different flavors.

Although the recipes were originally created by Florence Hanna for the restaurant, Ken's Foods is now a separate company from the steakhouse.

PART VI

THE NEW CLASSICS

Publick House

2002

The Publick House in Brookline's Washington Square was opened in 2002 by David Ciccolo. As far as classic Boston restaurants go, this is pretty recent. The Publick House is a beer restaurant and bar, patterned after those in the beer-centric country of Belgium. Although 2002 is not long ago for Boston restaurants, in terms of craft beer, 2002 may well have been eons ago. This means that craft beer, or beer in general, has seen a complete reversal during the time that the Publick House has been open.

Once upon a time, craft beer meant breweries such as Samuel Adams, Pete's Wicked Ale and Harpoon. Most American beers meant tasteless, mass-produced lagers from macro breweries such as Budweiser, Miller and Coors. Even though these breweries still make up the largest percentage of beer consumed, craft beer has shone like never before, or at least since local brewers provided the ale served at taverns during colonial days.

The region has seen an utter boom in craft beer during the last few years. Vermont breweries such as the Alchemist and Hill Farmstead have continued to put the Green Mountain State on the country's beer map. Massachusetts is home to Tree House Brewing Company from central Massachusetts, often regarded as the top brewery in the nation. Right here in Boston, Trillium Brewing Company is also one of the highest regarded breweries in the country.

The reason that these facts are important is because the Publick House predated these Massachusetts craft beer stalwarts. Granted, the Publick House's beer emphasis is on Belgian and European beer, but beer fans have been flocking to this restaurant as someplace much different from a normal bar for years, before the deluge of microbreweries. Trillium Brewing has such a strong reverence for Publick House that it named an IPA (India pale ale) after it, called the Publick House IPA, which can at times be found on draft. This also demonstrates Publick House's influence, as the ability to find Trillium on draft outside one of its own establishments is like finding Bigfoot in the wild.

Publick House is much more than a bar with a fantastic beer selection. The food is incredible. As with the beer, the focus of the food is Belgian. Favorite menu options include the mussels and fries (moules frites), which is a common Belgian dish. For anyone who has been to Belgium, this dish will make you feel as if you are dining in Bruges or Antwerp and not Brookline. Other dishes that the restaurant is known for include the meatloaf and mac and cheese. For beer, expect an extensive menu with about two hundred choices among draft, cans and bottles. In 2004, the Publick House expanded to include the Monk's Cell, which is a section of the establishment that serves only Belgian beers. The interior is dark with a bit of a cavernesque atmosphere. If you are looking for a newer classic Boston restaurant, make sure to check out the Publick House.

Craigie on Main

2002/2008

C raigie on Main, owned and operated by chef Tony Maws, is one of the most well-regarded restaurants in the Boston area. Craigie on Main began as a tiny basement bistro in the far reaches of Harvard Square; it was then known as the Craigie Street Bistrot. Located at 5 Craigie Street—which currently houses the restaurant Forage and prior to that 10 Tables Cambridge—Craigie Street Bistrot earned rave reviews soon after opening. It was only open certain nights of the week. It was quite a prize to earn a coveted table at the eatery.

In 2008, the business switched Cambridge neighborhoods and changed its name to Craigie on Main. It kept the recognizable "Craigie" moniker, but its new name described its current geography, on Main Street. The new address at 853 Main Street in Central Square could accommodate more diners than the Bistrot ever could.

What did not change with the move was Maws's reputation for crafting fine French-inspired dishes, which landed him "Best Chef" accolades from the likes of the James Beard Foundation, with the restaurant often earning high marks from local and national publications such as the *Boston Globe*, *Bon Appetit* and *Boston Magazine*. Overall, the dining experience at Craigie is upscale, with options including prix fixe multi-course meals. Adventurous culinary creations include tail-to-snout pig and fin-to-tail fish preparations. Chef Maws creates delicacies out of little-used parts of the animal. Chef, cookbook author and television star Andrew Zimmern gives rave reviews to the restaurant.

The menu is French influenced, as Maws trained in Lyon, France. It focuses on local and the freshest ingredients. Sample items may include octopus, duck or roasted chicken. Whatever is on the menu will be delicious. Chef Maws honed his craft in the kitchens of some of the most respected Boston-area chefs, including Ken Oringer at his famed restaurant Clio in the Back Bay and Steve Johnson at the Blue Room in Cambridge's Kendall Square (which was among Julia Child's favorite Cambridge restaurants). Maws also worked in San Francisco, Santa Fe and the aforementioned Lyon, France. Originally from Newton, Massachusetts, he opened Craigie not far from his hometown. He also was the owner of the Kirkland Tap and Trotter for almost six years in nearby Somerville.

Although Craigie on Main is an upscale restaurant with creative cuisine, white linen tablecloths and tasteful décor, it is also known for its bar, called COMB (get it, Craigie on Main Bar?), and here is the location of the one dish that has cemented Craigie in the annals of Boston culinary genius: the burger. Chef Maws originally started making the burger after moving to the current location. He wanted it to be something special, handcrafted to perfection, similar to the other menu choices. This burger has such a reputation that customers line up before dinner time to reserve their spot at Craigie. With only eighteen of these made each night, being able to sink your teeth into a Craigie burger is like searching for Atlantis.

The patty is made of Hardwick grass-fed beef (from Hardwick, Massachusetts) and includes a variety of different cuts of beef in it. It also consists of bone marrow and dried miso powder. It's placed on a lush but firm sesame seed bun. The cheese is cheddar from Shelburne Farms in Shelburne, Vermont. There is even a special Craigie ketchup that Chef Maws concocted. This burger has quite a reputation. It has earned the distinction of best burger in the city in multiple publications. Craigie also has an outpost in the Time Out Market located at the Landmark Center on Park Drive in the Fenway neighborhood. The burger is available there too but, again, on a very limited, first-come, first-served basis. As a specialty at COMB, Craigie recently offered a variety of specialty burgers served at various times.

Epilogue

With a city as steeped in history—and we're just talking culinary history—as Boston, clearly each and every classic Boston restaurant cannot fit into this volume alone. Hopefully though, this title presents a well-rounded edible tour of Beantown. From the earliest days of colonial Boston through the modern era, the "city upon a hill" that Governor John Winthrop preached about as a shining beacon is rooted in the past but at the same time looks to the future, with its heart firmly planted in the present. The same goes for its culinary scene. Dishes that this city is known for, including scrod, Boston baked beans and oysters, can still be found on menus today.

Union Oyster House, the original classic Boston restaurant. *Courtesy of Joseph Milano.*

Restaurants such as the Union Oyster House, Parker's Restaurant and the Bell in Hand Tavern have been around longer than many states have been part of the Union. Boston's many styles of cuisine are reflective of the makeup of its population. From the predominantly Italian North End to Chinatown to the Irish pubs scattered around the city, ethnicity and eateries go hand in hand. Along with the city itself, the surrounding towns of the South Shore, North Shore and MetroWest have their own specialties: the roast beef sandwich, fried clams and bar pizza. In addition, Boston also has many "new" classics, including favorites such as Craigie on Main and the Publick House. Boston is a foodie's paradise, with new eateries popping up seemingly weekly, but the establishments in this book are tried and true. They are simply classic Boston restaurants. From fine dining to snack bars, pubs to clam shacks, Boston's classic restaurants do not fit one particular mold. They are as unique as the city itself.

Bibliography

Ayto, John. *The Diner's Dictionary: Word Origins of Food and Drink*. Oxford: Oxford University Press, 2012.

Berkowitz, Roger, and Jane Doerfer. *The New Legal Sea Foods Cookbook*. New York: Broadway Books, 1993.

Bradford, William. *Of Plymouth Plantation: 1620–1647*. Edited by Samuel Eliot Morison. New York: Alfred A. Knopf, 1966.

Cain, Jacqueline. "Update: Amrheins Reopens This Weekend." *Boston Magazine*, February 12, 2016.

"Chelsea: The Perfect Bagel." WCVB: Chronicle. July 13, 2018.

Coleman, John R. *Blue-Collar Journal: A College President's Sabbatical*. Philadelphia: Lippincott, Williams and Wilkins, 1974.

Coombs, Linda. "Wampanoag Foodways in the 17th Century." *Plimoth Life*, 2005.

Curtin, Kathleen, and Sandra Oliver. *Giving Thanks: Thanksgiving Recipes and History from Pilgrims to Pumpkin Pie*. New York City: Clarkson Potter Publishers, 2005.

Ebben, Paula. "'Wild and Woolly' Combat Zone Just a Part of Storied Past in Boston's Chinatown." WCVB News, November 15, 2019.

Edelman, Larry. "Bull & Finch, the Inspiration for 'Cheers,' Finds Continued Success 50 Years Later." *Boston Globe*, June 5, 2019.

History.com Editors. "Armenian Genocide." History.com A&E Television Networks, October 1, 2010. www.history.com/topics/world-war-i/armenian-genocide.

Houton, Jacqueline. "How the Famous Hood Milk Bottle Arrived in Fort Point." *Boston Home*, Fall 2020.

Kearnan, Scott. "The Ultimate Guide to Chinatown." *Boston Magazine*, February 2019.

"Kowloon Stands Tried and True in Saugus." WCVB Chronicle, October 23, 2018.

Lawrence, J.M. "William Wong, 88; Restaurateur Who Built Kowloon in Saugus." *Boston Globe*, August 10, 2011.

Lynds, John. "Santarpio's Pizza Lands at Logan." *East Boston Times Free Press*, March 13, 2020.

Miller, Bryan. "Oh, to Dine in Saugus, Mass." *New York Times*, April 6, 1988.

Morgenroth, Lyna. *Boston Neighborhoods: A Food Lover's Walking, Eating and Shopping Guide to Ethnic Enclaves in and Around Boston*. Guilford, CT: Globe Pequot, 2001.

Morris, Jerry. *The Boston Globe Guide to Boston*. Guilford, CT: Globe Pequot, 2001.

Negri, Gloria. "Ralph Pocari, 84, Owned Popular Coffee Shop in the North End." *Boston Globe*, October 29, 2010.

Patkin, Abby. "Anna's to Close Friday in Honor of Owner's Passing." Wicked Local: Cambridge, February 13, 2019.

Patriot-Bridge Staff. "Living History in Charlestown: Warren Tavern Has Been a Local Mainstay Since 1780." *Charlestown Patriot-Bridge*, August 16, 2012.

Phantom Gourmet. Created by David and Dan Andelman, WSBK-TV, 1993–2021.

Phantom Gourmet Guide to Boston's Best Restaurants. New York: St. Martin's Press, 2006.

Rajewski, Genevieve. "Harvest." ArchitectureBoston 14, no. 1 (Spring 2011). architectureboston.wordpress.com/2011/02/03/harvest.

Schaffer, Mat. "Chinese Eatery Celebrates 50th Anniversary." *Boston Herald*, November 29, 2000.

Shuman, Cary. "Just Plain Great: Katz Bagel Bakery Pleasing Customers Since 1938." *Chelsea Record*, October 27, 2011.

Siegel, Elisha. "Not Your Bubby's Brisket Part II: An Exploration of Boston's Jewish Deli Scene." WGBH.org, February 3, 2018. www.wgbh.org/dining-out/2018/02/13/not-your-bubbys-brisket-part-ii-an-exploration-of-Bostons-jewish-deli-scene.

Southworth, Susan, and Michael Southworth. *AIA Guide to Boston*. Guilford, CT: Globe Pequot, 1992.

Speed, Kellie. "Slice of Life: The Best Bar Pizza Joints on the South Shore." *South Shore Living*, December 2017.

State Street Trust Company. *Taverns and Stagecoaches of New England*. Vol. 2. Boston: Rand Press, 1954.

Tong, Sophia W. "Joseph Bartley, Founder of Bartley's Burgers, Dies at 87." *Harvard Crimson*, March 22, 2018.

Trahan, Erin. "New Literary Group Turns History of Boston's Legendary 'Saturday Club' on Its Head." WBUR radio program, March 24, 2017. www.wbur.org/artery/2017/03/24/bostons-new-saturday-club.

Wachter, Paul. "A Little Taste of Armenia." *ONE Magazine*, July 2006.

Wilking, Alex. "Boca Grande Has New Owner and an Upcoming Cambridge Spot." *Boston Magazine*, July 12, 2016.

Wilson, Susan. *Heaven by Hotel Standards: The History of the Omni Parker House*. Boston: Omni Parker Publishing, 2014.

Winslow, Edward. "A Letter Sent from New England." In *A Journal of the Pilgrims at Plymouth*, edited by Dwight B. Heath. New York: Corinth Books, 1963.

Wolfson, John. "The Burrito War." *Boston Magazine*, May 15, 2006.

Wood, William. *William Wood's New England Prospect*. London: Tho. Gates, 1634.

Wright, Chris. "A Brief History of Plough & Stars." *Boston Phoenix*, August 30–September 6, 2001.

Zagat Boston Restaurants 2014. New York: Zagat Publishing, 2013.

WEBSITES

Websites for the restaurants were referenced.

About the Author

Jocelyn Moschella.

Zachary Lamothe is the author of the books *A History Lover's Guide to the South Shore*, *Connecticut Lore: Strange, Off Kilter and Full of Surprises* and *More Connecticut Lore: A Guidebook to 82 Strange Locations*. He has contributed to many in-print and online publications, and he runs the travel blog *Backyard Road Trips*. Zack lives in Massachusetts with his wife, two sons, dog and cat.